The Big Book of Christian Growth

Gospel Light

How to Make Clean Copies from This Book

You may make copies of portions of this book with a clean conscience if

- you (or someone in your organization) are the original purchaser;

- you are using the copies you make for a noncommercial purpose (such as teaching or promoting your ministry) within your church or organization;

- you follow the instructions provided in this book.

However, it is ILLEGAL for you to make copies if

- you are using the material to promote, advertise or sell a product or service other than for ministry fund-raising;

- you are using the material in or on a product for sale; or

- you or your organization are not the original purchaser of this book.

By following these guidelines you help us keep our products affordable.

Thank you,

Gospel Light

Permission to make photocopies or to reproduce by any other mechanical or electronic means in whole or in part any designated* page, illustration or activity in this book is granted only to the original purchaser and is intended for noncommercial use within a church or other Christian organization. None of the material in this book may be reproduced for any commercial promotion, advertising or sale of a product or service. Sharing of the material in this book with other churches or organizations not owned or controlled by the original purchaser is also prohibited. All rights reserved.

*Pages with the following notation can be legally reproduced: © 2001 Gospel Light. Permission to photocopy granted. *The Big Book of Christian Growth*

Editorial Staff

Publisher, William T. Greig • **Senior Consulting Publisher,** Dr. Elmer L. Towns • **Publisher, Research, Planning and Development,** Billie Baptiste • **Managing Editor,** Lynnette Pennings, M.A. • **Senior Consulting Editor,** Wesley Haystead, M.S.Ed.• **Senior Editor, Biblical and Theological Issues,** Bayard Taylor, M.Div. • **Senior Advisor, Biblical and Theological Issues,** Dr. Gary S. Greig • **Editorial Team,** Deborah Barber, Mary Gross, Sheryl Haystead • **Contributing Editors,** Amanda Abbas, David Arnold, Cinda Lasinski • **Senior Designer,** Lori Hamilton

Contents

Contents

Rock-Solid Discipleship

Have you ever tried to stare down a group of glassy-eyed preteens who refused to respond to your best attempts at engaging them in discussion? If so, this book is for you!

Preteens are capable of tremendous learning when their minds are engaged—when they are motivated to think, analyze and apply the principles of Scripture to their lives. But it's not always easy to lead them in animated discussions. Resistant kids can quickly reduce an unprepared teacher to despair! And sometimes even the most prepared teacher runs out of good discussion questions, suddenly finding that the mental "question file" is filled with blank cards!

The Big Book of Christian Growth is filled with activities and discussion starters that will transform your students from glassy-eyed listeners to kids excited about finding out what the Bible has to say about their lives! But that's not all—we've provided you with over 300 meaty, relevant questions guaranteed to get your kids thinking, talking and applying Scripture in ways meaningful to them!

The foundation for this book is 17 Scripture passages with important discipleship concepts for preteens. We added dozens of discussion questions based on kids' lives, and mixed in 75 generic active games, quiet games and activities, and instant activities, you can use with any of those topics. The result: rock solid discipleship for preteens.

Make every moment with your preteens count. With the help of *The Big Book of Christian Growth*, you'll never be at a loss for something relevant to talk about!

Ways to Use This Book

Identify Your Purpose: What Do You Need?

Here are just a few of the many ways to use the resources in this book.

Customized Curriculum for a Special Purpose

Thinking of starting a small group Bible study, discipleship weekend, retreat, camp or a new midweek program? The possibilities are endless, and the Bible content is all here!

Curriculum Supplement for Existing Program

Does your curriculum let kids focus on fun to the detriment of their spiritual development? Supplement your regular Bible study or Sunday School curriculum to be sure students are getting their full "nutritional quotient" of Scripture application.

Time Stretchers and Transition Activities

Don't let those teachable moments be lost to chaos! While waiting for parents or standing in line, pull out a Discussion Card related to the topic or passage you've been studying. Pick an Instant Activity (pp. 55-71), get your students involved and turn those minutes into a learning event!

Family Devotions

Take family devotions to a new level! Play a game together or use an activity to help your family discuss a Scripture passage. Read a discussion starter card at mealtime as a way to start talking about an absorbing topic. Use discussion starter cards while traveling in the car to stave off boredom! Make every moment count while helping kids think through and apply God's Word to their lives!

Choose Your Topic

Check out the Discussion Card topics listed in the table of contents. Read the Bible passages listed and choose one that fits your focus. Photocopy and cut apart the cards you will use (follow the directions on p. 73).

Choose Your Activity Level

Based on the space available (large or small? indoor or outdoor? furniture or not?), choose the kind of activity you need: an active game, a quiet game or activity, or a quick and easy-to-use instant activity. (If you have the space and plenty of helpers, a variety of activities from which students choose can help motivate participation and keep interest high.)

Choose Your Activities

Find the section listing the kinds of activities you have in mind, and pick as many as you need! It's that simple.

•

Tips for Guiding Discussions with Preteens

Preteen students are full of thoughts and ideas! Sometimes those thoughts and ideas come pouring out (whether or not they relate to the topic at hand) and other times it seems as though nothing you do will get your students to open up and talk with you.

One-Word Answerers

Some students seem to be only one-word answerers! Your one-word answerer may find it difficult to speak up in a crowd or may lack confidence in his or her ability to give the right answer. Keeping discussion groups small (no more than six to eight students) will give you the opportunity to interact with and encourage each student.

If a student gives a too-short or one-word answer to a question, be ready with several follow-up questions to motivate further response. **What might you do instead? Why do you think your idea is good? What might be the results of your action?**

Nonstop Talkers

Other students are nonstop talkers! Your nonstop talker may just be so enthusiastic that he or she can't help but answer all the questions. Structured discussion activities help by giving all students an opportunity to talk without having to remind your nonstop talkers to give others a turn.

Silly Answerers

Occasionally students decide to be silly instead of fulfilling an activity's intended purpose. It is usually wise not to make a major issue out of such behavior. Students may be feeling apprehensive or self-conscious. When possible, laugh along with them for a few moments. Once you have smiled together, then you can redirect students to the reason for the activity. Asking students to write their responses on paper may help them focus on the task, rather than on each other.

Off-Course Conversations

If students show a significant interest in whatever drew the group off track AND if you feel that topic has real value to the group, you may decide to leave your lesson plan and stay with the new issue.

However, if a complete change of direction is not warranted, use new or restated questions to bring attention back to the topic and its particular implications. Restate the original question to remind students of the issue at hand. Or move on to a new question if you feel the students have probably said all they are likely to contribute to the previous question.

Difficult Discussions

The Discussion Cards included in this book bring up everyday situations in which kids usually have some measure of control. However, students may want to talk about some other types of current events (kidnappings, murders, natural disasters, etc.). When students want to talk about these types of situations, help students think about specific ways they can rely on God. Emphasize that while most of us will never find ourselves in such situations, God's love and care are always present.

Some students may have problems or fears they'd like to discuss in private. Invite students to speak with you after class. If you become aware of a problem that needs intervention (homelessness, abuse, hunger, etc.), in private alert your supervisor or pastor as soon as possible. Be careful not to embarrass students by discussing their private problems openly either in class or with other adults.

Active Games
Tips for Fun Active Games

1. State the purpose of the game ("to help us learn more about . . . ," "to help us think of ways to . . . ," etc.), focusing on what is to be learned or expressed, not just on the game itself.

2. Be prepared with all the materials needed for your games. Students are likely to start misbehaving if you are unprepared with materials or confused about instructions or procedures.

3. In team games some students may become impatient with less coordinated members of their team. Before the game, let students know that (catching and tossing the ball) can be difficult and that all students will need to practice and help each other in order to be successful. During the game, your own posi-tive comments will discourage rude remarks, or put-downs.

4. If a student announces "I don't want to do this!" or has difficulty getting started on an activity, the best approach is a matter-of-fact response. "It's OK to watch for a while." After a few minutes, again try inviting the student to participate in the activity.

5. Make sure the game area is cleared of any obstacles. Remove any area rugs that could be tripped over or fragile items that could be broken.

6. Because students this age value the opinions of their peers so highly, deal with discipline problems individually. Avoid embarrassing the student in front of friends. Talk with him or her alone to redirect the student's behavior.

Active Games
Candy Cups

Materials
- [ ] Bibles
- [ ] Discussion Cards for Bible passage you select (prepared as instructed on p. 73)
- [ ] 15 paper cups
- [ ] individually wrapped pieces of candy
- [ ] pennies

Preparation
Place cups together as shown in sketch and place one piece of candy and a Discussion Card in each cup.

Introduction
Guide volunteers to read aloud the Bible passage you selected. Students refer to Bible passage during the activity.

Procedure
1. Students stand approximately 4 feet (1.2 m) from cups. Give pennies to students. Students take turns attempting to toss a penny into a cup. If penny lands in a cup, student receives the candy after reading and responding to the card in the cup.

2. Student returns card to cup and adds another piece of candy to the cup. Continue until everyone has had a chance to read a Discussion Card and receive candy.

Teaching Tips
1. Small boxes of raisins, or tokens which can be used for obtaining a snack item, can be used instead of wrapped candy.

2. If students have difficulty tossing pennies into cups, invite students to stand closer to the cups.

3. For large groups, provide one or more choices of snack items and do not place candy in cups. Students form teams. Volunteers from each team toss their pennies simultaneously. Volunteers return to their teams with the Discussion Cards. Each team writes responses on the back of their card. The team finishing first reads Discussion Card and response aloud and gets first choice of snack items.

Active Games
Chair Share

Materials

- ☐ Bibles
- ☐ Discussion Cards for Bible passage you select (prepared as instructed on p. 73)
- ☐ one chair for every two students
- ☐ index cards
- ☐ marker
- ☐ tape

Preparation

Place chairs in a circle. Make two sets of identically numbered index cards, a different number for each chair. Tape one set of numbered index cards onto backs of chairs.

Introduction

Guide volunteers to read aloud the Bible passage you selected. Students refer to Bible passage during the activity.

Procedure

1. Two students sit on each chair. Students move from chair to chair according to the directions you give. ("If you are wearing blue, move two chairs to the left." "If you came to church in a car, move three chairs to the right." "If you ate cereal for breakfast, move one chair to the right." "If you made your bed this morning, move two chairs to the left.") If there are too many students to sit on one chair, they must at least put their hands on the chair.

2. After giving several directions, call out a number. Students sitting on or touching that chair select and answer a Discussion Card. Repeat as time permits.

Teaching Tips

1. Instead of chairs, tape sheets of construction paper onto the floor. Students stand on papers or place at least one foot on the sheet of paper.

2. If space is limited, cover table with butcher paper. For every two students, draw a circle on the paper. Number the circles. Give each student a game marker to place on a circle. Students move game markers according to your directions.

Active Games
C.H.O.I.C.E.

Materials

☐ Bibles
☐ Discussion Cards for Bible passage you select (prepared as instructed on p. 73)
☐ large sheet of paper
☐ marker
☐ masking tape
☐ beanbag
☐ large container

Preparation

Draw a line down the center of a large sheet of paper. Letter "Team 1" on one side and "Team 2" on the other. Display in classroom. Make a masking-tape line about 4 feet (1.2 m) from large container.

Introduction

Guide volunteers to read aloud the Bible passage you selected. Students refer to Bible passage during the activity.

Procedure

1. Divide class into two teams. Teams stand behind masking-tape line and take turns attempting to toss beanbag into a container. Each time beanbag lands in container, team writes a letter of the word "choice" on its side of paper.

2. When one team completes the word, a volunteer selects a Discussion Card that describes a situation and reads card aloud to the team. Volunteers from the team tell at least three different choices that a student in that situation could make. Other team tells which choice they think would be best and why. Repeat game as time permits.

Teaching Tip

For variety, divide the group into teams by a new method. Try one of the following:

1. Students line up in alphabetical order according to the first letter of first names. Divide the line into two equal teams.

2. Students group themselves by a color on their clothes (blue) or the kind of shoe they are wearing (sneaker).

3. Students line up in order of the last digit of their phone numbers. Divide the line into two equal teams.

Enrichment Idea

To make the game move faster, use a beanbag for each team.

Active Games
Circle Jump-Up

Materials
☐ Bibles
☐ Discussion Cards for Bible passage you select (prepared as instructed on p. 73)
☐ a chair for each student

Preparation
Arrange chairs in a circle.

Introduction
Guide volunteers to read aloud the Bible passage you selected. Students refer to Bible passage during the activity.

Procedure
1. One student volunteers to be "It" and stands in the middle of the circle of chairs. All other students sit in chairs. Remove the extra chair.

2. "It" chooses one of the Discussion Cards and reads the situation and/or question aloud. One or two volunteers sitting in the circle tell answers. Then call out, "Who can be wise?" "It" answers, "all the boys," "all the girls" or "everyone." Students who are named jump up to trade chairs while "It" tries to sit down on a chair also. Student who is left without a chair is "It." Repeat as time permits.

Teaching Tip
Lead students to discuss their answers by asking questions such as, **When has this happened to you? What might happen next? What else could you do?**

Enrichment Idea
Invite "It" to vary the categories when naming students who must trade chairs (e.g., "everyone wearing green," "everyone with blond hair," "everyone with brown eyes").

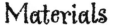

Clean-Sweep Relay

Materials

☐ Bibles
☐ Discussion Cards for Bible passage you select (prepared as instructed on p. 73)
☐ two brooms
☐ unshelled peanuts

Introduction

Guide volunteers to read aloud the Bible passage you selected. Students refer to Bible passage during the activity.

Procedure

1. Divide class into two teams. Teams line up with half of each team on opposite sides of the room and the other half on the other side. Give each team one broom and place several unshelled peanuts on the floor near broom. At your signal, the first person on the half of the team with the broom sweeps the unshelled peanuts to the other side of the room and then gives the broom to the first person in line on the other half of his or her team. Team members continue sweeping unshelled peanuts from one side of the room to the other until all team members have had a turn.

2. Volunteer from team that finishes relay first chooses and reads a Discussion Card for the other team to answer.

Teaching Tip

Provide additional peanuts for students to snack on after completing relay.

Crazy Relay

Materials

☐ Bibles

☐ Discussion Cards for Bible passage you select (prepared as instructed on p. 73)

☐ index cards

☐ markers

Preparation

Write five silly instructions on separate index cards. (Count backward from 10 to 1. Shake the hands of two other people. Sing "Row, Row, Row Your Boat." Bark like a dog. Do six jumping jacks.) Add five Discussion Cards and then mix up and stack cards. Make a stack of cards for each team of four or five students.

Introduction

Guide volunteers to read aloud the Bible passage you selected. Students refer to Bible passage during the activity.

Procedure

Group students into two teams. Students line up on one side of the room. Place stacks of cards opposite each team on the other side of room. First player of each team takes an instruction from the top of the stack belonging to his or her team, returns to the team and performs the action or answers the question(s) on the card. Then the next player takes his or her turn. The first team to complete all its cards wins. Winning team chooses a Discusson Card for other team to answer. Repeat the game again as time permits.

Teaching Tips

1. If you have a small group, play the game all together.

2. To play this game quietly, have students mime their silly actions. Even if you don't need to be quiet, students will enjoy this variation.

3. You may wish to invite a parent or other adult to help supervise this activity.

Determination Squares

Materials

- ☐ Bibles
- ☐ Discussion Cards for Bible passage you select (prepared as instructed on p. 73)
- ☐ markers
- ☐ index cards
- ☐ masking tape

Preparation

Make direction labels from index cards as shown in sketch. Tape Discussion Cards and labels to floor, forming a game board (see sketch).

Introduction

Guide volunteers to read aloud the Bible passage you selected. Students refer to Bible passage during the activity.

Procedure

1. Give each student an index card and a marker. On index card each student writes two instructions consisting of a number between one and four and a direction, such as "2-North; 3-West." Mix index cards together and put them in a pile.

2. Students stand around the game board, with each student choosing the closest Discussion Card as his or her starting square. One at a time, students select direction cards and move to the squares indicated by the directions on the cards. (For example, if a student selects a card which reads "2-North; 1-East," he or she would move, from his or her starting square, two squares north and one square east (see sketch).

3. Student reads the Discussion Card he or she lands on and tells an answer. Student then returns to his or her place around the game board. Continue until each student has had at least one turn or until time is called.

Teaching Tips

1. If the directions on an index card lead a student off the game board, he or she stops at the last paper on the game board.

2. If time in class is limited, prepare the direction cards ahead of time.

3. For groups of more than six students, create two game boards and play games simultaneously. In small groups, students have many opportunities to participate and teachers are able to build friendships. If you don't have a teacher for each small group, consider asking parent volunteers to assist periodically.

Active Games
Foiled Juggling

Materials
- ☐ Bibles
- ☐ Discussion Cards for Bible passage you select (prepared as instructed on p. 73)
- ☐ aluminum foil
- ☐ marbles
- ☐ children's music cassette/CD and player

Preparation
Loosely wrap several sheets of foil around a marble to make a foil ball. Make two additional foil balls without marbles. Make one set of three balls for each group of eight to ten students.

Introduction
Guide volunteers to read aloud the Bible passage you selected. Students refer to Bible passage during the activity.

Procedure
1. Students form groups of no more than 10 students. Each group of students stands in a circle. Students count off and then reform the circle in mixed-up order. Give foil ball to student Number 1. Number 1 passes a foil ball to Number 2. Number 2 passes the ball to Number 3 and so on. Continue passing the ball until students are familiar with the pattern.

2. Add additional foil balls to circle. As you play music, students pass all the foil balls by following the pattern. When you stop the music, students holding foil balls open up the balls to find the one with the marble. Student who has the marble reads and answers a Discussion Card. Other volunteers tell additional ways to respond to the question. Make balls again and continue game as time and interest allow.

Teaching Tips
1. If space is limited or if students begin to throw balls, students must sit on the floor or around a table and pass the balls.

2. If a student who has already described a situation receives the ball with the marble, he or she passes the ball to the nearest student who has not had a turn.

Active Games
Hopscotch Rocks

Materials

☐ Bibles

☐ Discussion Cards for Bible passage you select (prepared as instructed on p. 73)

☐ masking tape

☐ index cards

☐ marker

☐ three game markers for each student

Preparation

Use masking tape to make a Hopscotch pattern and toss line on the floor. Write numbers on index cards and place in Hopscotch pattern as shown in sketch.

Introduction

Guide volunteers to read aloud the Bible passage you selected. Students refer to Bible passage during the activity.

Procedure

1. Give each student three game markers. Students stand in a line at one end of the Hopscotch pattern. First student tosses game markers onto the Hopscotch pattern and adds up the numbers in the blocks the markers land on. (If a marker lands outside of pattern, the number is zero. If a marker lands on more than one number, use the higher number.) Student then hops through grid to pick up his or her game markers and goes to the end of the line. Repeat with remaining students in line.

2. Student with the highest number reads a Discussion Card and chooses a volunteer to respond to the question on the card. Repeat game as time permits.

Teaching Tip

Have students take one step back with each toss to make the game more challenging.

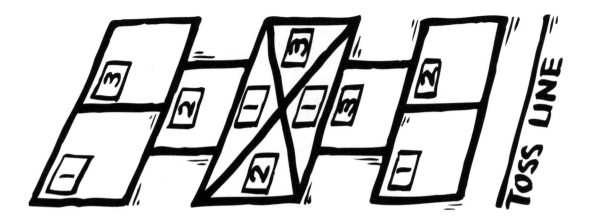

Human Tic-Tac-Toe

Materials

- ☐ Bibles
- ☐ Discussion Cards for Bible passage you select (prepared as instructed on p. 73)
- ☐ masking tape
- ☐ index cards
- ☐ marker
- ☐ slips of paper
- ☐ paper bag

Preparation

On the floor, make a masking-tape Tic-Tac-Toe grid with sections large enough for students to stand in. On index cards, write the numbers 1 to 9, one number on each card. Place one card in each section. Also write numbers on small slips of paper and place slips of paper in a paper bag.

Introduction

Guide volunteers to read aloud the Bible passage you selected. Students refer to Bible passage during the activity.

Procedure

1. Divide class into two equal teams.
2. One player on first team reads a Discussion Card. Volunteers from his or her team tell responses. Then student takes a slip of paper from bag and stands on the corresponding section on the Tic-Tac-Toe grid. (Students may use their own bodies as markers by holding arms to form Xs or Os.)
3. Continue playing with teams taking turns, until one team gets three players in a row. Repeat game as time permits.

Teaching Tips

1. If your class has 15 or more students, make two or more grids and play the games simultaneously or make a 16-square grid—a team must get four players in a row to win.
2. If your class is small, students place construction-paper markers in the grid.

Active Games
Keep It Moving!

Materials

- ☐ Bibles
- ☐ Discussion Cards for Bible passage you select (prepared as instructed on p. 73)
- ☐ a chair for each student
- ☐ small index cards
- ☐ marker
- ☐ children's music cassette/CD and player

Preparation

Arrange chairs in a circle, with seats facing outward. (If you have more than six to eight students, make two circles.) Number each chair by writing numbers on index cards and placing a card under each chair. Make a duplicate set of number cards.

Introduction

Guide volunteers to read aloud the Bible passage you selected. Students refer to Bible passage during the activity.

Procedure

As you play music, students walk around the circle of chairs (see sketch). When you stop the music, each student sits on a chair. Choose a number from the duplicate set of number cards. Student sitting on that chair chooses one of the Discussion Cards and reads it aloud. Volunteers tell ways to respond to the question on the card.

Teaching Tips

1. If you have a large group, you may choose more than one number each time you stop the music.

2. Discuss responses to cards that describe situations by asking, **When have you been in a situation like this? What happened? What might some kids feel like doing in this situation? Which of these responses is a way of showing love for God and others?**

Enrichment Ideas

1. Write a variety of instructions on separate index cards: "Read and answer a card." "Do six jumping jacks." "Thumb wrestle with a partner." Each instruction may be used more than once. Number the cards and place each one under a chair. When you choose a number from the set of number cards, student sitting on that chair follows the instruction on the card under the chair.

2. Instead of using chairs, students tape numbered construction-paper squares to the floor to make a path. Students follow the path instead of walking around chairs.

Active Games
Knock It Down

Materials

☐ Bibles
☐ Discussion Cards for Bible passage you select (prepared as instructed on p. 73)
☐ Styrofoam cup
☐ masking tape
☐ newspaper

Preparation

Place cup on the floor with stack of Discussion Cards behind it. Make a 10-foot (3-m) masking-tape line 6 to 8 feet (1.8 to 2.4 m) from the cup.

Introduction

Guide volunteers to read aloud the Bible passage you selected. Students refer to Bible passage during the activity.

Procedure

1. One student volunteers to be the Guard and stands about 6 inches (15 cm) in front of the cup. All other students stand behind the masking-tape line.

2. Give each student several sheets of newspaper to crumple into balls. At your signal, students throw their newspaper balls at the cup. The Guard uses hands and feet to keep the balls from knocking over the cup.

3. When a student knocks over the cup, call "Freeze." Student who knocked over cup reads a question from a Discussion Card for the Guard to answer. Discuss the answers by asking, **What are some other ways to answer this question? Why?** Then the Guard trades places with the student who knocked over the cup. Students collect newspaper balls. Play the game until at least several students have had a turn to be the Guard. After playing the game, students should wash hands to remove newsprint from hands.

Teaching Tips

1. To make the game more challenging, group students in a circle, placing the Guard and cup in the middle of the circle. Students stand approximately 6 feet (1.8 m) from the cup.

2. If you have more than eight students, play two games simultaneously.

3. You may wish to set a time limit of about 10 seconds for each round of throwing newspaper balls.

6 ft (1.8m)

Active Games
Mark the Spot

Materials

- ☐ Bibles
- ☐ Discussion Cards for Bible passage you select (prepared as instructed on p. 73)
- ☐ masking tape
- ☐ small slips of paper
- ☐ markers
- ☐ blindfold

Preparation

Place a small masking-tape X in the center of the room. Make sure the area is clear of any obstacles that students could trip over. Use masking tape to make a starting line at one end of the room.

Introduction

Guide volunteers to read aloud the Bible passage you selected. Students refer to Bible passage during the activity.

Procedure

1. Give each student a small slip of paper and a marker. Each student writes his or her name on the paper and attaches a piece of tape to it.

2. Students stand at starting line. Blindfold the first player. Player turns around a few times, walks to where he or she thinks the X is located and tapes his or her paper to the floor. Continue until each student has had a turn.

3. The student whose paper is closest to the X selects a Discussion Card to read to the group. Volunteers tell responses. Continue game as time permits, each time placing the X in a different spot.

Teaching Tip

If you have a large group, divide class into groups of four or five to play game and divide cards among each group.

•

On-the-Way Relay

Materials

- ☐ Bibles
- ☐ Discussion Cards for Bible passage you select (prepared as instructed on p. 73)
- ☐ masking tape
- ☐ chairs
- ☐ large sheets of construction paper

Preparation

Use masking tape to make a starting line on one side of the classroom. On the other side of the room, place one chair for each team of four to six students.

Introduction

Guide volunteers to read aloud the Bible passage you selected. Students refer to Bible passage during the activity.

Procedure

1. Divide class into teams of four to six. Teams line up behind starting line. Give the first student in each line two sheets of paper. Students "travel" across the room, around the chairs and back, stepping only on their sheets of construction paper and moving paper for each new step. Students hand papers to the next person in line who then continues the relay. Play until everyone has had a turn to travel.

2. A volunteer from the first team to complete the relay reads and answers a Discussion Card. Repeat relay as time permits.

Teaching Tips

1. Substitute large paper grocery bags for construction paper.

2. Remember to give your own answer to some of the questions on Discussion Cards. Your personal example is the best teacher.

3. When students read a card with a situation, ask several of the following questions to extend the conversation: **What are some other ways to respond to a situation like this? How could a kid your age show God's love in this situation?**

Active Games
Post-it Pandemonium

Materials
- ☐ Bibles
- ☐ Discussion Cards for Bible passage you select (prepared as instructed on p. 73)
- ☐ pencils
- ☐ Post-it Notes
- ☐ children's music cassette/CD and player

Introduction
Guide volunteers to read aloud the Bible passage you selected. Students refer to Bible passage during the activity.

Procedure

1. Students number off. Give each student a Post-it Note and a pencil. Each student writes his or her number on a Post-it Note. Students then randomly place notes around the room in unusual but visible places.

2. Students walk randomly around the room as you play music. After a few moments, stop the music. Each student quickly finds and puts a hand on a Post-it Note. (Only one person may touch each note.) Call out a number. Student touching note with that number reads aloud the question on a Discussion Card. Call out a second number. Student with hand on second number answers the question or asks a volunteer to answer. Repeat activity using other cards as time permits.

Teaching Tips

1. This game will work equally well with small groups and large groups. However, in larger groups, you may wish to call out more than one number after each question is read in order to have more than one student answer each question at a time.

2. If time is limited, make up Post-it Notes ahead of time and place them around the room yourself.

3. If your room is too small or if students are too active, students remain stationary and pass the Post-it Notes while the music is playing. (You may wish to use index cards instead of Post-it Notes.)

Active Games
Seek 'n' Find

Materials
☐ Bibles
☐ Discussion Cards for Bible passage you select (prepared as instructed on p. 73)
☐ blindfolds (one for each student)

Introduction
Guide volunteers to read aloud the Bible passage you selected. Students refer to Bible passage during the activity.

Procedure
1. Students form pairs. Place Discussion Cards facedown in a stack. Teacher or volunteer chooses the top card and reads it aloud. Pairs discuss and decide on an answer, and then choose two keywords of their answer.

2. Students stand in a circle, with students on opposite sides of the circle from their partners. Give each student a blindfold. Students put on blindfolds. At your signal, pairs try to find each other by calling out the keywords of their answers and by trying to recognize each other's voices. The first pair to find each other tells answer to the question. (Students remove blindfolds once the first pair has found each other.)

3. Form new pairs and read another Discussion Card. Continue playing game as time permits.

Teaching Tips
1. Blindfolds may be made by ripping or cutting an old sheet into 12×36-inch (30.5×91.5-cm) strips. Fold strips in half twice (lengthwise) and tie around students' heads. Students may also help each other tie blindfolds around heads.

2. Make sure game area is cleared of any obstacles. Remove any area rugs that could be tripped over.

Alternate Idea
For small groups, select one student to be "It." "It" reads aloud one Discussion Card. Secretly, each student, including "It," thinks of an answer. "It" is blindfolded. While other students move around the classroom, "It" calls out "Answer!" Each student must say a keyword from his or her answer at two-second intervals. "It" tries to tag any student. After a student is tagged, remove the blindfold from "It." "It" reads the Discussion Card again and the tagged student tells his or her full answer.

Shoe Search Relay

Materials

☑ Bibles

☑ Discussion Cards for Bible passage you select (prepared as instructed on p. 73)

Introduction

Guide volunteers to read aloud the Bible passage you selected. Students refer to Bible passage during the activity.

Procedure

1. Students remove shoes and place them in a pile in the middle of the room. Divide class into two teams. Teams line up on opposite sides of the room. First student on each team describes his or her shoes to the second student on the team. Second student runs to the shoe pile to find the correct shoes and gives them to the first student who puts on the shoes and goes to the end of the line. Second student on each team then describes his or her shoes to the third person in line. Continue until all students have their shoes. If a student picks up the wrong shoes, he or she must go back to find the correct shoes.

2. Volunteer from team that finishes relay first chooses and reads a Discussion Card for the other team to answer.

Teaching Tip

Before playing game, be sure that play area is free of sharp objects that might hurt students' feet.

Active Games
Sticky Ball

Materials

- ☐ Bibles
- ☐ Discussion Cards for Bible passage you select (prepared as instructed on p. 73)
- ☐ masking tape
- ☐ double-sided tape
- ☐ sponge or other lightweight ball
- ☐ blindfold

Preparation

Tape Discussion Cards onto wall, door or bulletin board, forming a grid (see sketch).

Introduction

Guide volunteers to read aloud the Bible passage you selected. Students refer to Bible passage during the activity.

Procedure

1. Help students wrap double-sided tape around the ball to make a sticky ball. Blindfold the first player. He or she stands 3 to 4 feet (.9 to 1.2 m) from the cards. Gently turn the player around several times. Player holds out the sticky ball and walks to the grid of cards, fastening the ball onto one of the cards. (If ball does not touch a card, use the card nearest to where the ball touched.)

2. Player removes blindfold, reads aloud the card the ball is stuck to and answers the question on the card. Continue as time permits.

Teaching Tips

1. If you have more than six to eight students in your group, make more than one grid and sticky ball.

2. If a soft ball is not available, wrap double-sided tape around several pieces of crumpled paper to make a sticky ball.

Enrichment Idea

Write a number (100, 200, 300, etc.) on each card. When the sticky ball is attached to the card, the player is awarded that number of points. You may wish to award bonus points to players who tell more than one answer.

Simplification Ideas

1. Instead of using a sticky ball, blindfolded player holds out a hand as he or she walks to the grid of cards. Player tells an answer to the card his or her hand touches.

2. Place cards on floor. Players toss beanbags onto the cards.

Active Games
Straw Relay

Materials

☐ Bibles

☐ Discussion Cards for Bible passage you select (prepared as instructed on p. 73)

☐ plastic drinking straws

☐ 1½-inch (3.45-cm) paper squares

Preparation

Place Discussion Cards in a pile on one side of the room.

Introduction

Guide volunteers to read aloud the Bible passage you selected. Students refer to Bible passage during the activity.

Procedure

1. Group students into two teams. Teams line up across the room from the Discussion Cards. Give each student a straw and a paper square. The first player on each team puts straw in his or her mouth, picks up the paper square by sucking through the straw and brings the paper square to the other side of the room. Each player takes a turn.

2. Volunteer from team that gets all its paper squares to the other side of the room first chooses a Discussion Card, reads the card aloud and answers the question. Continue the activity as time permits.

Teaching Tips

1. Let students practice carrying the paper squares before starting the relay.

2. For more of a challenge, create an obstacle course through which students must move while carrying the paper squares.

3. As you play each round of this relay, vary the process by which teams are formed. For the first round, allow students to group themselves into teams. Then for the second round, announce that the person on each team who is wearing the most (red) should rotate to another team. Then do the relay again. As you repeat the relay, vary the method of rotation so that teams are composed of several different students each time.

Active Games
Take Aim!

Materials
- ☐ Bibles
- ☐ Discussion Cards for Bible passage you select (prepared as instructed on p. 73)
- ☐ several rubber bands

Introduction
Guide volunteers to read aloud the Bible passage you selected. Students refer to Bible passage during the activity.

Procedure
1. Students place Discussion Cards that describe situations in rows facedown on the floor at one side of the classroom.

2. Students stand on other side of the classroom. Give a rubber band to first student. Student shoots rubber band into the air so that it lands on or near one of the Discussion Cards. Student removes the card from the floor, reads the situation and tells a way to show obedience to the Bible passage you are studying in that situation. Student places card back on the floor before next student takes a turn. Repeat activity, giving each student a turn.

Teaching Tip
Bring several rubber bands to class in case one breaks. However, give only one rubber band to a student at a time.

Enrichment Idea
Letter points ranging from 10 to 50 on cards. Students earn points as they play game. (Optional: Student receives an additional 10 points if he or she can ricochet rubber band off the ceiling onto a card.)

Alternate Idea
Instead of using a rubber band, number each card from one to six. (Numbers may be repeated.) Each student takes a turn to roll a number cube, choosing a card that is numbered the same as the number he or she rolls.

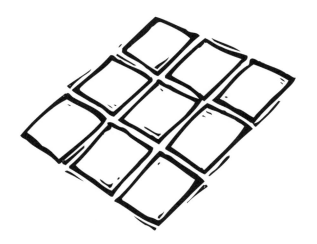

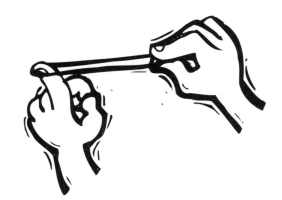

Team Bowling

Materials

- ☐ Bibles
- ☐ Discussion Cards for Bible passage you select (prepared as instructed on p. 73)
- ☐ 10 empty soda cans or milk cartons
- ☐ ball
- ☐ optional—paper and pencil

Preparation

Set up cans or cartons to represent bowling pins as shown in sketch.

Introduction

Guide volunteers to read aloud the Bible passage you selected. Students refer to Bible passage during the activity.

Procedure

Divide group into teams of three or four students each. First player stands approximately 10 feet (3 m) from the bowling pins. Player rolls a ball to see how many pins he or she can knock down and then reads aloud one of the Discussion Cards. Player's team tells ways to respond to the question on the card. The number of responses must be the same as the number of pins knocked down. (Optional: Teams also record a point for each pin knocked down.) Repeat with players from each team.

Teaching Tips

1. If space is limited, use paper cups and a small rubber ball on a tabletop.
2. Assign two students to be ball retrievers. One student stands at each end of the line of bottles and is responsible for retrieving the ball when it lands on his or her side.

Enrichment Idea

Students write their own questions to use in the game.

Discipline Tip

Position yourself next to a student who has a hard time controlling his or her behavior. Then you'll find it easier to privately redirect misbehavior by putting a hand on the student's shoulder or quietly saying, **Jeremy, wait till the pins are set up before you bowl.**

Active Games
Three-Ball Toss

Materials
- [ ] Bibles
- [ ] Discussion Cards for Bible passage you select (prepared as instructed on p. 73)
- [ ] a variety of balls and Frisbees
- [ ] large box
- [ ] construction paper
- [ ] masking tape

Preparation
Place balls and Frisbees in box. Set up a baseball diamond using construction paper as bases. Tape bases securely in place approximately 10 feet (3 m) apart. Place box next to home plate.

Introduction
Guide volunteers to read aloud the Bible passage you selected. Students refer to Bible passage during the activity.

Procedure
1. One student stands on home plate and acts as the batter. Another student acts as catcher and stands near box. The remaining students stand in the field. The batter chooses a Discussion Card and answers the question on it.

2. Batter then selects three objects from the box and throws them into the field in rapid succession. He or she tries to run completely around diamond, touching each base, before the students in the field return all three objects to the catcher who puts objects into the box.

3. Select a second student to be the batter and play game again.

Teaching Tips
1. If possible, play this game outside using carpet squares or towels for bases.

2. Balls to use might include playground balls, basketballs, volleyballs, tennis balls, beach balls or Ping-Pong balls. If playing indoors or if space is limited, use balls made from crumpled foil or paper or use sponge balls.

3. If students are throwing objects too far, change the rules of the game so that students throw balls and Frisbees backwards over their shoulders.

4. You may wish to make a rule that only two students may stand and field objects thrown inside the baseball diamond while other students stand and field objects thrown outside the diamond. Following these guidelines will help students in the field avoid collisions with the runner.

5. Adjust size of diamond if needed to make it possible for a student to get back to home base while objects are being retrieved.

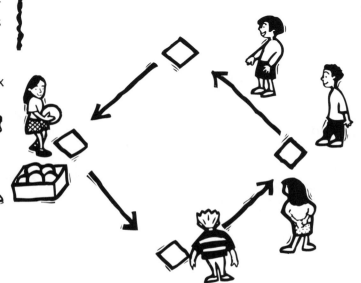

The Big Book of Christian Growth •

Towel 'n' Ball Toss

Materials

- ☐ Bibles
- ☐ Discussion Cards for Bible passage you select (prepared as instructed on p. 73)
- ☐ masking tape
- ☐ two beach (or large bath) towels
- ☐ volleyball or 9-inch (23-cm) rubber ball

Preparation

Use masking tape to make a line dividing the playing area in half.

Introduction

Guide volunteers to read aloud the Bible passage you selected. Students refer to Bible passage during the activity.

Procedure

1. Divide class into two teams. Teams stand on either side of the dividing line. Two to four volunteers from each team form a group. Give each group a towel. Students hold the corners of their towels.

2. Give one group a ball. Group uses towel to toss the ball over the dividing line where it is caught on the towel of the other group (see sketch). Groups continue catching and tossing the ball over the line, trying to see how many times they can cross the line. When the ball falls on the floor, play stops. The team on the side where the ball lands reads and answers the question on a Discussion Card.

3. After giving a response, the team starts the ball again with a different group holding towels. Continue playing game as time permits, reading and answering several Discussion Cards.

Teaching Tips

1. If possible, play this game outdoors with a volleyball net. Give each pair of students a towel and use water balloons instead of a volleyball or rubber ball.

2. All partners must hold onto the towel at all times.

3. You may need to mark outside boundaries—areas where the ball should not be tossed.

4. If space is limited, students use dish towels and a foam ball.

5. If you have a large group, bring more towels and make additional playing courts.

Water-Pass Relay

Materials

- Bibles
- Discussion Cards for Bible passage you select (prepared as instructed on p. 73)
- two pitchers of water
- four chairs
- two bowls
- two empty plastic soda or water bottles

Introduction

Guide volunteers to read aloud the Bible passage you selected. Students refer to Bible passage during the activity.

Procedure

1. Divide class into two teams. Teams line up on one side of the playing area. Place a pitcher of water on a chair in front of the first student in each line and an empty bowl on a chair at the end of each line.

2. Give first student in each line an empty plastic soda or water bottle. First student fills the bottle with water from pitcher, places his or her thumb over the top of the bottle mouth and then turns the bottle upside down and passes it. Each player may use only his or her thumb to keep the water in, keeping the bottle upside down at all times. The last player pours the water into the empty bowl, runs to the front of the line, refills the bottle and starts it down the line again. Teams continue until one team fills empty bowl. (Replenish water pitchers as necessary.)

3. Volunteer from team that finishes relay first chooses and reads a Discussion Card for the other team to answer.

Teaching Tips

1. Play relay outdoors.

2. If you have a large group, form additional teams of no more than 10 students each.

Quiet Games and Activities
Tips for Great Quiet Games and Activities

1. Help students get started by doing the activity with them. This not only helps students understand the game's rules and the purpose, but it is also a powerful model.

2. Be sure to give your own answers to some of the questions on the Discussion Cards. Talk about your failures as well as your successes. Your real-life examples may be the best-remembered part of a lesson!

3. Make sure to have your activity and materials ready ahead of time. Don't waste class time looking for materials or trying to figure out how to do an activity. Preparing ahead of time allows you to use all your class time focusing on the students instead of on other things. Giving your attention to your students is a great way to show God's love!

4. Listen attentively to the answers students give. Use eye contact, nod in response, or comment on an idea. To help students listen more effectively to each other, ask the rest of the class follow-up questions that connect to a student's answer, such as, **How would Robert's idea have worked in a situation you have been in?**

5. In responding to the Discussion Cards, some students may quickly respond with a negative response. Often these responses are attention-getting devices, reflecting the desire of juniors to appear "cool" to their peers. Instead of correcting the student, it often works to comment with a smile, **That's the first thing we might all think of doing. But what other choices are there in this situation?**

Add-On Answers

Materials

- ☐ Bibles
- ☐ Discussion Cards for Bible passage you select (prepared as instructed on p. 73)
- ☐ marker
- ☐ slips of paper
- ☐ small paper bag
- ☐ large sheets of paper

Preparation

Write the numbers 5 through 10 on separate slips of paper and place in paper bag.

Introduction

Guide volunteers to read aloud the Bible passage you selected. Students refer to Bible passage during the activity.

Procedure

1. Volunteer selects and reads aloud a Discussion Card that describes a situation. Another student then selects a slip of paper from the number bag. Student begins writing on a large sheet of paper a way to respond to the situation, using only the number of words indicated on the slip of paper. Students take turns selecting numbers and adding words to the description until answer is complete.

2. Continue with other Discussion Cards and large sheets of paper as time permits. Use the following questions to guide students in discussing ways to respond to situations:

   - **What are some other choices kids could make in this situation?**
   - **What are some reasons kids might make one of these choices?**
   - **What is another choice that might be better than the one we wrote? Why?**

Alternate Idea

Instead of writing answers, tape-record students speaking.

Teaching Tip

Some students may "go blank" when faced with saying something in only a given number of words! To help a student get started, suggest, **Write down the main word of your idea. Add other words before and after the main word until you've used the number you were given. The other people who draw a number will add to your words until they think your idea is finished.**

> I would talk to my sister and tell her that I was really the one who had left

Advice Column

Materials

- ☐ Bibles
- ☐ Discussion Cards for Bible passage you select (prepared as instructed on p. 73)
- ☐ several newspapers or magazines
- ☐ scissors
- ☐ paper
- ☐ pencils

Preparation

Cut out several age-appropriate advice columns from newspapers or magazines.

Introduction

Guide volunteers to read aloud the Bible passage you selected. Students refer to Bible passage during the activity.

Procedure

1. Divide class into groups of two or three. Give each group paper, pencils and a Discussion Card that describes a situation.

2. Allow students several minutes to look at newspaper or magazine advice columns. Then invite students to suggest and vote on a name for their own advice column (e.g., Dear Gabby, Dear Nosealot, Dear Willie and the Wiseguys, Dear Dr. Helpzout). Groups write letters from people in the situations described on their Discussion Cards.

3. Invite a volunteer from one group to read aloud group's letter. Other students tell advice they would give to someone in that situation to help them show obedience to the Bible passage you read. Repeat with remaining groups. If time permits, distribute new Discussion Cards and repeat activity.

Answer Match

Materials

- ☐ Bibles
- ☐ Discussion Cards for Bible passage you select (prepared as instructed on p. 73)
- ☐ large Post-it Notes
- ☐ pencils
- ☐ coin

Introduction

Guide volunteers to read aloud the Bible passage you selected. Students refer to Bible passage during the activity.

Procedure

1. Divide class into four groups. Give each group a Discussion Card. Give each student a Post-it Note and pencil. On the Post-it Note, each student writes an answer to his or her group's Discussion Card.

2. After students have written answers, invite volunteers to read Discussion Cards aloud. Collect Post-it Notes and arrange them on one end of the table in a grid. Students stand on the other side of the table and take turns tossing a coin onto the grid and guessing which question is answered on the note the coin lands on. Reread Discussion Cards as needed. Extend the conversation by asking, **What are some other ways to answer that question?**

Teaching Tips

1. Instead of reading Discussion Cards aloud, print questions and/or situations from four Discussion Cards on a large sheet of paper.

2. Instead of Post-it Notes, you may wish to use index cards or construction paper squares. (If using large sheets of construction paper, you may wish to have students toss a beanbag.)

Alternative Idea

One group of students hides answers around classroom. The other group searches for the answers and then guesses which question each student answered. Second group hides its answers for first group to find. Continue discussion as suggested above.

Calendar Toss

Materials

☐ Bibles

☐ Discussion Cards for Bible passage you select (prepared as instructed on p. 73)

☐ calendar page for the current or upcoming month

☐ button or coin

Introduction

Guide volunteers to read aloud the Bible passage you selected. Students refer to Bible passage during the activity.

Procedure

1. Place calendar page on one end of table. Each student takes a turn to toss a button or coin two times onto the numbered squares of the calendar page. Student adds up the two numbers on which the button or coin lands to determine his or her score. At the end of each round, the student with the highest score reads aloud one of the Discussion Cards. Student with the next highest score answers the question on the card.

2. Repeat activity with students reading and answering other cards as time permits.

Teaching Tip

If you have a large class, photocopy calendar page to make one copy for each group of four to six students. Students play game and discuss cards in small groups.

Enrichment Idea

Students make and decorate individual prayer calendars for the upcoming month. On each day of the month students write people or things to pray for such as names of other students in the class, teacher, pastor, church activities, missionaries, friends at school, etc. Provide markers, glitter pens, scissors, glue and used greeting cards for students to use in decorating their calendars. Students take calendars home.

DECEMBER

Sun.	Mon.	Tues.	Wed.	Thurs.	Fri.	Sat.
1	2	3	4	5	6	7
8	9	10	11	12	13	14
15	16	17	18	19	20	21
22	23	24	25 ★	26	27	28
29	30	31				

Cartoon Creations

Materials

- ☐ Bibles
- ☐ Discussion Cards for Bible passage you select (prepared as instructed on p. 73)
- ☐ 12×18-inch (30.5×45.5-cm) sheets of construction paper
- ☐ scissors
- ☐ ruler
- ☐ markers

Preparation

Cut the construction paper into 4×18-inch (10×45.5-cm) strips, one for each student or pair of students.

Introduction

Guide volunteers to read aloud the Bible passage you selected. Students refer to Bible passage during the activity.

Procedure

Give each student or pair of students a strip of paper and a Discussion Card that describes a situation. Students draw four-frame cartoons showing the situation and what the person in that situation might decide to do. (In order to divide strip of paper into four frames, student folds paper in half and then in half again.) Volunteers read Discussion Cards and show cartoons they created.

Teaching Tip

Display cartoons on bulletin board.

Quiet Games and Activities
Celebrity Interviews

Materials

☐ Bibles
☐ Discussion Cards for Bible passage you select (prepared as instructed on p. 73)
☐ index cards
☐ marker

Introduction

Guide volunteers to read aloud the Bible passage you selected. Students refer to Bible passage during the activity.

Procedure

1. Students name famous people (movie stars, basketball players, talk show hosts, etc.). As students respond, print names of people on index cards. Shuffle cards.

2. Students take turns first selecting a Discussion Card that describes a situation and then choosing a card with the name of a famous person. Students answer questions on

Discussion Cards according to advice they think their famous person would give a kid in the situations. Ask the following questions to evaluate their responses and extend the conversation.

- **Why do you think** (name of famous person) **would give this advice?**
- **What do you think** (name of famous person) **might value most?**
- **How might most kids your age answer the question on the card?**
- **What are some other ways that you could respond to that situation?**

Teaching Tip

It's best for you to take the role of the "celebrity interviewer," so you can ask questions and guide the conversation.

Enrichment Idea

Videotape or record students' interviews.

Family Talk

Materials
☐ Bibles
☐ Discussion Cards for Bible passage you select (prepared as instructed on p. 73)

Introduction
Guide volunteers to read aloud the Bible passage you selected. Students refer to Bible passage during the activity.

Procedure
1. Divide class into two groups. Assign one group to be parents and the other group to be students.

2. Invite a volunteer to choose a Discussion Card that describes a situation and read it aloud. Each group discusses the situation on the card and thinks of a helpful way to react or respond to the situation. Students in parent group should think of answers that parents would give; students in student group think of answers kids their age would give.

3. After several minutes, invite volunteers from both groups to tell how they would respond to the situation. Discuss each situation using the following questions. Repeat activity with different cards.

   • **When have you or someone you know been in a situation like this? What happened?**

   • **What do you think would be the result of your suggested action?**

   • **What is another good way to respond to this situation?**

Teaching Tips
1. Groups switch roles before selecting new cards.

2. Groups should be limited in size to four to six students. In a large class, assign more than one group to each role.

Go-Fer Game

Materials

- ☐ Bibles
- ☐ Discussion Cards for Bible passage you select (prepared as instructed on p. 73)
- ☐ two baskets
- ☐ 16 slips of paper
- ☐ pencils
- ☐ butcher paper
- ☐ scissors
- ☐ measuring stick

Preparation

Place Discussion Cards in one basket. Number slips of paper from 1 to 16 and place them in the other basket. Cut butcher paper into 3-foot (.9-m) squares, making one for each team of three or four students.

Introduction

Guide volunteers to read aloud the Bible passage you selected. Students refer to Bible passage during the activity.

Procedure

1. Divide group into teams of three or four students each. Give each team a pencil and a butcher-paper square. Teams fold paper squares in half four times and then unfold paper to reveal 16 squares. Teams number the squares randomly from 1 to 16, writing the numbers small in the corners of squares (see sketch).

2. Choose one number from the basket, read the number aloud and set it aside. That is the square to be used for the first round. Then each team chooses one player to be the Go-fer. The Go-fer chooses a Discussion Card

from the basket, brings it back to his or her team and reads the card aloud. Team decides how to respond to the question and writes its idea in the designated square. After one minute, call time. Go-fers return cards to the basket. Begin the next round, following the same procedure. Play continues until one team has filled in four squares in a row. Winning team reads its responses aloud. Repeat game as time permits.

Teaching Tips

1. If you will have time to play the game more than once, make additional butcher paper squares ahead of time.

2. If a team gets the same card more than once, team must write a different answer.

3. If time is short, begin the game by choosing three numbers from the basket. Teams write "FREE" in the designated squares.

Enrichment Idea

Vary the conditions for winning (responses must be written in each of the four corners, any four connecting squares, etc.).

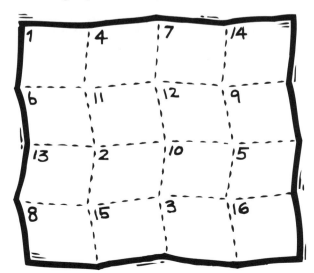

Quiet Games and Activities
Guest Talk

Materials

☐ Bibles
☐ Discussion Cards for Bible passage you select (prepared as instructed on p. 73)

Preparation

Invite one or more college students or young adults to come to your class to answer questions on Discussion Cards. Choose several Discussion Cards that describe situations for guest(s) to discuss. Give cards to your guest(s) ahead of time and ask your guest(s) to be prepared to tell about times they have been in situations similar to the ones described on the Discussion Cards.

Introduction

Guide volunteers to read aloud the Bible passage you selected. Students refer to Bible passage during the activity.

Procedure

1. Invite guest(s) to read one of the Discussion Cards you selected and to take two or three minutes to tell about a time he or she was in a similar situation.

2. Invite students to ask guest(s) questions about the situations discussed. Ask students these questions to extend the conversation:

   • **When are some times you have been in situations like this? How did you feel?**

   • **What do you know about God that would help you in a situation like this?**

Teaching Tips

1. Some college students or young adults may not have had much experience talking with children. Be sure to let your speaker(s) know what to expect from the students in your class. Also review what kinds of details and stories are appropriate for your students to hear. Encourage each speaker to keep stories as brief as possible.

2. Before the speaker(s) arrives, review with students the polite ways to ask questions. Make a brief list of guidelines such as, listen when others talk and raise your hand if you wish to speak.

Age-Level Tip

Older elementary students still see adulthood as a far-off event in their lives, but becoming a teenager—that's something they are looking forward to! Listening to a high school student, college student or young adult tell about his or her situation is far more real and interesting to a preteen than listening to a person of his or her parents' age.

Match Up

Materials
- Bibles
- Discussion Cards for Bible passage you select (prepared as instructed on p. 73)
- index cards
- pencils

Introduction

Guide volunteers to read aloud the Bible passage you selected. Students refer to Bible passage during the activity.

Procedure

1. Students form two teams and stand in single-file lines. Give each student an index card and a pencil. Place Discussion Cards facedown in a stack. The first student on each team selects a Discussion Card and reads aloud the question to his or her team. All members of the team, including the first player, write individual answers to the question without consulting each other.

2. First player collects cards from his or her team members and then reads answers aloud. Teams receive points for each answer by a team member that matches the first player's answer. (Variation: Teams receive points for each answer by a team member that is different from the first player's answer.)

3. The first players go to the ends of their lines. The next students are then the first players. Distribute more index cards and continue game, selecting new first players each time.

Teaching Tips

1. Instead of index cards, sheets of paper may be used. Students write their names on papers and number answers. Then use the paper for more than one round of the game.

2. For large classes, form additional teams.

3. For smaller classes, form only one team. Students get points for matching the first player's answer.

4. You or another student may act as a score-keeper.

Partner Concentration

Materials

- ☐ Bibles
- ☐ Discussion Cards for Bible passage you select (prepared as instructed on p. 73)
- ☐ index cards
- ☐ pencils
- ☐ scissors

Introduction

Guide volunteers to read aloud the Bible passage you selected. Students refer to Bible passage during the activity.

Procedure

1. Group students into pairs. Give each pair an index card, pencil and scissors. A volunteer chooses a Discussion Card and reads it aloud to all pairs. Pairs tell each other what they would do in that situation or how they would answer the question. Pairs write answers on index cards and then cut cards in half.

2. Collect all cards, mix them up and place them facedown on table or floor. Pairs play a game like Concentration, taking turns turning over two cards at a time to find cards that go together. After all cards have been matched, invite volunteers to read their cards.

3. Students change partners and repeat activity with different Discussion Cards.

Quiet Games and Activities
Pass and Switch

Materials
- ☐ Bibles
- ☐ Discussion Cards for Bible passage you select (prepared as instructed on p. 73)
- ☐ coin
- ☐ beanbag or other object to pass around (hat, paper cup, spoon, etc.)

Introduction
Guide volunteers to read aloud the Bible passage you selected. Students refer to Bible passage during the activity.

Procedure
1. Students stand in a circle. Volunteer stands outside of the circle and flips a coin, calling out which way the coin lands—heads up or tails up. For heads, students pass beanbag or other object clockwise. For tails, students pass object counterclockwise. Students continue passing object as volunteer flips coin and calls the direction at least five times and then says stop.
2. The person holding the object reads one of the Discussion Cards. Volunteers tell how they would respond. Continue as time permits.

Teaching Tips
1. Add additional objects to the circle after a few minutes. Each person holding an object after five direction changes reads a Discussion Card.
2. If students have difficulty flipping coins, suggest they simply toss coins in the air.

Quiet Games and Activities
Penny Pass

Materials
☐ Bibles
☐ Discussion Cards for Bible passage you select (prepared as instructed on p. 73)
☐ penny

Introduction
Guide volunteers to read aloud the Bible passage you selected. Students refer to Bible passage during the activity.

Procedure
1. Students sit in a circle. Volunteer sits in the middle of the circle with eyes closed. Give one student in the circle a penny. Students begin passing the penny. At your signal, volunteer opens his or her eyes while all students pretend to be passing the penny. Volunteer tries to guess who has the penny by calling out that person's name. When the volunteer guesses correctly (or after three incorrect guesses), he or she trades places with the person holding the penny.

2. Student who had the penny reads a Discussion Card that describes a situation and chooses another student to tell how he or she would respond to that situation. Continue playing game as time permits.

Enrichment Idea
To increase the challenge or if time is short, use two pennies. Both students with pennies tell how they would respond to situation described on Discussion Card. First student guessed sits in the middle for the next round of play.

Sentence Connections
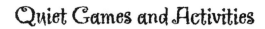

Materials
- ☐ Bibles
- ☐ Discussion Cards for Bible passage you select (prepared as instructed on p. 73)

Introduction
Guide volunteers to read aloud the Bible passage you selected. Students refer to Bible passage during the activity.

Procedure
1. Students sit in a circle. Invite a volunteer to read aloud a Discussion Card that describes a situation. Student to the right of volunteer tells a sentence that answers the question on the card. The next student also tells an answer, connecting his or her sentence to the previous sentence by using one of the words from that sentence. The word "I" may not be used as the connecting word. For example, if the first student says, "I would go with my friend to talk to the teacher," the second student may say a sentence using the word "talk." "I would talk to my friend about what we should do." Continue until each student has had a turn.

2. Repeat with other Discussion Cards as time permits.

Teaching Tip
In order to help students understand the activity, you may need to say the first sentence and a sentence that connects to it.

Quiet Games and Activities

Spin the Light

Materials
☐ Bibles
☐ Discussion Cards for Bible passage you select (prepared as instructed on p. 73)
☐ flashlight

Introduction
Guide volunteers to read aloud the Bible passage you selected. Students refer to Bible passage during the activity.

Procedure
1. Students sit in a circle. (Darken your classroom if possible.) Turn on the flashlight and place it in the middle of the circle. Volunteer chooses and reads a Discussion Card and then spins the flashlight. When the flashlight stops, student closest to the beam of light from the flashlight answers the question on the card. (Optional: Spin the flashlight for another student to answer the same question.)

2. Student who answered the question chooses and reads another Discussion Card and spins the flashlight. Continue with other cards as time permits.

Teaching Tips
An unlit candle may be used instead of a flashlight.

This Is a Fish

Materials
- Bibles
- Discussion Cards for Bible passage you select (prepared as instructed on p. 73)
- two small balls

Introduction
Guide volunteers to read aloud the Bible passage you selected. Students refer to Bible passage during the activity.

Procedure
1. Sit with students in a circle. Give a ball to the student on your right saying, "This is a fish." Student asks, "A what?" Reply, "A fish." Student then gives the ball to the next student and says, "This is a fish." Second student asks, "A what?" First student again asks you, "A what?" You say, "A fish." This information is passed on to the second student who then passes on the ball. Students continue asking and replying.

2. Once the first message is underway, add another ball, passing it to the left saying, "This is a horse" (or other animal). Students on the left question and reply in the same manner as those on the right. Students continue passing the two balls around the circle until one student ends up with both balls.

3. Student with both balls reads a Discussion Card and chooses another student to answer the question on the card. Repeat the passing game beginning with different volunteers each time.

Teaching Tips
1. Play a practice round to familiarize students with the rules and mechanics of the game.

2. This activity works best with at least eight students in each circle. If you have fewer than eight students in your class, use the Simplification Idea below.

Simplification Idea
Play music while passing an object around the circle. The student holding the object when the song is stopped reads a Discussion Card.

What's the Question?

Materials

- ☐ Bibles
- ☐ Discussion Cards for Bible passage you select (prepared as instructed on p. 73)
- ☐ index cards
- ☐ pencils
- ☐ children's music cassette/CD and player

Introduction

Guide volunteers to read aloud the Bible passage you selected. Students refer to Bible passage during the activity.

Procedure

1. Divide class into groups of three. Give each group a Discussion Card, a pencil and an index card. Each group reads its Discussion Card and writes an answer on its index card. Collect cards.

2. All students sit in a circle. As you play music, students pass one of the index cards around the circle. Stop the music after several moments. Student holding the card reads the answer and makes up a question that would go with the answer.

Teaching Tip

If student is unable to think of a question, allow him or her to ask several students for ideas. The student may then choose one of the suggestions as his or her question.

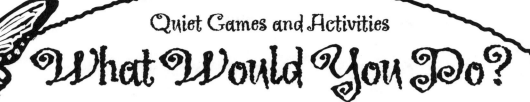

What Would You Do?

Materials

- ☐ Bibles
- ☐ Discussion Cards for Bible passage you select (prepared as instructed on p. 73)
- ☐ pencils
- ☐ paper

Introduction

Guide volunteers to read aloud the Bible passage you selected. Students refer to Bible passage during the activity.

Procedure

1. Students select partners. Give each pair paper and a pencil. Then read aloud a Discussion Card. Partners work together to list on paper as many different responses (positive and negative) as they can.

2. Then read the Discussion Card aloud again and invite pairs to tell the responses they listed. As each response is described, ask volunteers from the class to tell if they think the action would or would not show obedience to the Bible passage you read. Repeat with several other cards that describe situations.

- **How many different ways of acting in this situation can you think of?**

- **What do you think most kids would do?**

- **Have you ever been in a situation like this? What did you do?**

Enrichment Idea

Explain that the class will receive a point for each different response to a situation. Each student secretly predicts how many points they think the class will earn. (Optional: Tell students that if the total number of points matches or surpasses your own prediction, they will receive a snack. Keep your prediction well within the range of success.) Students write their predictions on paper, keeping the papers hidden.

As responses are read aloud, a volunteer records points on paper. Total the number of points. Each student compares his or her prediction. (Optional: Distribute snack item if the point total matches or surpasses your prediction.)

You Blew It!

Materials

- ☐ Bibles
- ☐ Discussion Cards for Bible passage you select (prepared as instructed on p. 73)
- ☐ butcher paper
- ☐ masking tape
- ☐ marker
- ☐ straws
- ☐ Ping-Pong ball

Preparation

Cover table with butcher paper, taping paper securely. Draw lines on the paper to divide it into sections, one section for each student. Tape a Discussion Card in each section.

Introduction

Guide volunteers to read aloud the Bible passage you selected. Students refer to Bible passage during the activity.

Procedure

1. Assign each student a section of the paper you prepared. Students sit or kneel around table near assigned sections.

2. Give each student a straw and place a Ping-Pong ball in the center of the table. Students rest arms on edge of table, creating a barrier to keep ball on table. Students blow through straws to make the ball move away from them. Students must remain seated or on knees. After about 15 seconds, call time. Students stop blowing.

3. Student in whose section the ball is located reads and answers Discussion Card. Continue playing as time permits.

Teaching Tips

1. If you do not have Ping-Pong balls, almost any light item will work (feather, cotton ball, small piece of Styrofoam packing material, etc.).

2. Instead of using straws to blow, students make fans by cutting paper plates in half and then wave the fans back and forth to make a wind.

Instant Activities
Tips for Engaging Instant Activities

1. Instant activities are easy to set up and are a fun way to review the Bible truth of any lesson. They can be used anytime and anyplace! Have one or two of these games on hand for those times when you run out of lesson plans before you run out of time or when what you planned to do doesn't work out.

2. To use the activities with specific Bible lessons, prepare Discussion Cards that go along with the topic of the lesson (see p. 73). Whenever you have some extra time with students, just pull out your Discussion Cards and follow the activity directions! Activities marked with ☀ need only Bibles and the Discussion Cards. The other activities require only a few other simple materials.

3. To make these activities even easier to use, photocopy pages 56-71, cut out the activities and glue the activity directions onto large index cards. Keep the activity cards in a card-file box along with your Discussion Cards.

4. Positive reinforcement—it's not just a bribe; it's noticing when a student is doing something right, and praising the student for it. Think about yourself: How do you feel when someone points out what you do right? How do you feel when someone only points out what you do wrong? Make an effort to offer words of praise to each student at least once during your class time.

☀ Active Alphabet

Materials
☐ Bibles
☐ Discussion Cards for Bible passage you select (prepared as instructed on p. 73)

Procedure
Students form groups of three or four. Call out a three-letter word ("hat," "dog," "mop," "ant," etc.). Each group quickly spells word with their bodies. Watch students and announce which group finishes forming the word first. Read a Discussion Card aloud. One or more students from the group that formed the word first tell answers to discussion question. Repeat with new three-letter words and different Discussion Cards.

Behind-the-Back Toss

Materials
☐ Bibles
☐ Discussion Cards for Bible passage you select (prepared as instructed on p. 73)
☐ soft ball or beanbag

Procedure
Students stand in a group. A volunteer reads one of the Discussion Cards aloud and then stands in front of the group with back facing the group. Students in group mix themselves up. Volunteer tosses soft ball or beanbag over shoulder. Student in group who catches the ball or beanbag answers question on Discussion Card. Repeat with other volunteers.

Instant Activities
Candy Toss

Materials

- ☐ Bibles
- ☐ Discussion Cards for Bible passage you select (prepared as instructed on p. 73)
- ☐ resealable plastic bag filled with individually wrapped candies

Procedure

Students stand in a circle. Read one of the Discussion Cards and toss the bag to a student. Student answers question, takes out one piece of candy and tosses bag to another student. That student tells his or her answer to question on Discussion Card and takes a piece of candy.

Continue until all students have taken a piece of candy from the bag, using a new Discussion Card question several times throughout the tossing. Students eat candy together.

Instant Activities
Card Toss

Materials

- ☐ Bibles
- ☐ Discussion Cards for Bible passage you select (prepared as instructed on p. 73)
- ☐ large container (wastepaper basket, bucket, etc.)

Preparation

Place large container in the center of the room.

Procedure

Give each student a Discussion Card. Students fold cards in half and then stand about 4 feet (1.2 m) from container. Students take turns toss-ing cards into the container. When a card lands in the container, student reads and answers that Discussion Card. Continue as time permits.

Chair Trade

Materials

☐ Bibles

☐ Discussion Cards for Bible passage you select (prepared as instructed on p. 73)

☐ chairs

Preparation

Arrange chairs in a circle.

Procedure

Students sit in chairs. Close your eyes. While you count slowly to three, students randomly trade chairs. Keeping your eyes closed, call out the name of one of your students. The student sit-ting to the right of the student whose name you called reads and answers one of the Discussion Cards. Repeat, calling other students' names.

☀ Circle Count

Materials

☐ Bibles

☐ Discussion Cards for Bible passage you select (prepared as instructed on p. 73)

Procedure

Students stand in a circle and begin counting around the circle. Whenever someone comes to a number with a three or seven, that student chooses and answers a Discussion Card. (Note: If the same students keep answering, have students change places in the circle or choose different numbers.)

Instant Activities
☀ Circle Spin

Materials
☐ Bibles
☐ Discussion Cards for Bible passage you select (prepared as instructed on p. 73)

Procedure
Students stand in a circle. Volunteer stands in the middle of the circle with eyes closed. Volunteer spins around several times, stops and points. Whichever student the volunteer is pointing at reads and answers one of the Discussion Cards. Repeat activity with other volunteers.

Instant Activities
Coin Cups

Materials
☐ Bibles
☐ Discussion Cards for Bible passage you select (prepared as instructed on p. 73)
☐ paper cups
☐ pennies

Procedure
Divide class into pairs. Give each student a cup and a penny. Invite a volunteer to read a Discussion Card aloud. Students place pennies in cups. Call "Heads" or "Tails." Students turn cups over so that pennies fall out onto table or floor. Each student whose penny shows the side called tells his or her partner how he or she would answer the question on the Discussion Card. If both students' pennies are showing the named side, both students tell answers. If neither students' pennies are showing the named side, students place pennies into cups and play again. Invite several volunteers to tell answers to the whole class. Repeat with other Discussion Cards.

Container Bounce

Materials

☐ Bibles

☐ Discussion Cards for Bible passage you select (prepared as instructed on p. 73)

☐ large container

☐ playground ball

Procedure

Students stand approximately 3 feet (.9 m) from a container. Students take turns bouncing a ball, attempting to get ball into container. If the ball goes into the container, student reads and answers one of the Discussion Cards.

☀ Count Around

Materials

☐ Bibles

☐ Discussion Cards for Bible passage you select (prepared as instructed on p. 73)

Procedure

Students sit in a circle. Tell students a number between 2 and 25. Starting with any student, students count from 1, standing up to say their numbers and continuing around the circle until the number you chose is reached. Student who says the chosen number reads and answers one of the Discussion Cards. Repeat, naming another number and starting with a different student.

Instant Activities
Discussion Dots

Materials
- Bibles
- Discussion Cards for Bible passage you select (prepared as instructed on p. 73)
- marker
- large sheet of paper

Preparation
Draw a row of 15 dots across a large sheet of paper.

Procedure
Students take turns crossing off either one or two dots. (It is not necessary for the dots to be next to each other.) Student who crosses off the last dot reads a Discussion Card aloud. Volunteers tell how they would answer the question on the card. Repeat the activity with another row of dots, discussing cards as time permits.

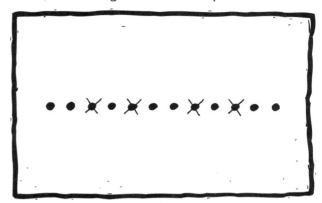

Instant Activities
Draw Straws

Materials
- Bibles
- Discussion Cards for Bible passage you select (prepared as instructed on p. 73)
- straws or paper strips
- scissors

Preparation
Cut straws or paper strips into equal lengths, one for each student. Cut one again so that it is shorter than the others.

Procedure
Hold straws or papers in your hand so that they look even. Each student takes a straw or paper. Student with the shorter straw or paper reads and answers one of the Discussion Cards.

Instant Activities
Fists

Materials
- ☐ Bibles
- ☐ Discussion Cards for Bible passage you select (prepared as instructed on p. 73)
- ☐ cardboard tube or baseball bat

Procedure
Choose two volunteers. Students take turns placing hands around a cardboard tube or baseball bat from bottom to top. The student whose hand ends up at the top reads and answers one of the Discussion Cards. Repeat with different volunteers as time permits.

Instant Activities
☀ Group and Regroup

Materials
- ☐ Bibles
- ☐ Discussion Cards for Bible passage you select (prepared as instructed on p. 73)

Procedure
Students walk around the room. Call out a number (from two to five). Group divides into groups of the number called. For example, if the number two is called, students stand in groups of two. Any student left without a group chooses and answers a Discussion Card. Repeat as time permits.

☀ Handy Pileup

Materials
☐ Bibles
☐ Discussion Cards for Bible passage you select (prepared as instructed on p. 73)

Procedure
One student puts a hand palm down on table or floor. The other students add their own hands one at a time to the pile. The hand on the bottom is withdrawn and added to the top of the pile. Continue until you signal stop. Student whose hand is on the bottom of the pile reads and answers one of the Discussion Cards. Repeat as time permits.

Hopscotch

Materials
☐ Bibles
☐ Discussion Cards for Bible passage you select (prepared as instructed on p. 73)
☐ masking tape
☐ children's music cassette/CD and player

Preparation
Use masking tape to outline a Hopscotch pattern on the floor.

Procedure
As you play music, all students hop one after the other through the pattern. When music stops, students freeze. Student who is standing in or closest to the first square reads and answers one of the Discussion Cards. Repeat as time permits.

Instant Activities
Hot Potato

Materials
- ☐ Bibles
- ☐ Discussion Cards for Bible passage you select (prepared as instructed on p. 73)
- ☐ small object to pass around (marker, eraser, glue stick, etc.)
- ☐ children's music cassette/CD and player

Procedure
Students pass object around the table as you play music. When music stops, student holding the object picks a Discussion Card from the pile and reads it aloud. Student tells answer before asking one other student to answer the card as well. Repeat as time permits.

Instant Activities
Musical Chairs

Materials
- ☐ Bibles
- ☐ Discussion Cards for Bible passage you select (prepared as instructed on p. 73)
- ☐ chairs
- ☐ children's music cassette/CD and player

Preparation
Place two rows of chairs back-to-back, with one less chair than number of students.

Procedure
Play music. Students walk around chairs in time to the music. When music stops, students quickly sit on chairs. Student left standing answers question on one of the Discussion Cards or selects another person to answer the question. Play again as time permits with other students and Discussion Cards.

Instant Activities
☀ Number Guess

Materials
☐ Bibles

☐ Discussion Cards for Bible passage you select (prepared as instructed on p. 73)

Procedure
Read one of the Discussion Cards. Secretly choose a number from zero to five. Students stand with hands behind their backs. At your signal, students guess number by showing number of fingers. Each student whose guess matches that of the teacher answers question from Discussion Card.

Instant Activities
☀ Odd or Even

Materials
☐ Bibles

☐ Discussion Cards for Bible passage you select (prepared as instructed on p. 73)

Procedure
Divide class into pairs. One student chooses "odd" and the other chooses "even." Each student puts a hand behind his or her back and together they count "One, two, three." On "three," both students thrust a hand in front of them with one to five fingers showing. If the total number of fingers is odd, the player who chose "odd" selects and reads a Discussion Card.

If the total is even, the other player selects a card. Volunteers answer question on card.

Instant Activities
☀One, Two, Buckle My Shoe

Materials
☐ Bibles

☐ Discussion Cards for Bible passage you select (prepared as instructed on p. 73)

Procedure
Students sit in a circle. First student selects a Discussion Card and tells his or her shoe size. Students begin passing the card facedown around the circle, counting off until the number of the first student's shoe size is reached. The person who has the card when that number is reached reads the card aloud and answers the question on the card. Continue with other cards as time permits.

Instant Activities
Over/Under

Materials
☐ Bibles

☐ Discussion Cards for Bible passage you select (prepared as instructed on p. 73)

☐ children's music cassette/CD and player

☐ small object to pass around (marker, eraser, etc.)

Procedure
Students stand in a line. As you play music, the first student passes object over his or her head, the second student passes it between his or her legs, and so on to the end of the line. Last student in line brings object to the front of the line and continues passing object. When the music stops, student holding the object chooses and answers a Discussion Card. Continue as time permits.

Instant Activities
Penny Flip

Materials
☐ Bibles
☐ Discussion Cards for Bible passage you select (prepared as instructed on p. 73)
☐ pennies

Procedure
Divide class into groups of no more than four. Give each group a penny. Read aloud one of the Discussion Cards. At your signal, one person in each group flips coin. Groups whose coins are heads answer question on the Discussion Card. Continue flipping coins and discussing cards as time permits.

Instant Activities
☀ Ring Around the Teacher

Materials
☐ Bibles
☐ Discussion Cards for Bible passage you select (prepared as instructed on p. 73)

Procedure
Students stand in a circle around you. Students walk around the circle while you slowly count to 10 with your hand outstretched. When you say "10," student closest to your hand reads and answers a Discussion Card.

Instant Activities
☀Rock, Paper, Scissors

Materials
☐ Bibles
☐ Discussion Cards for Bible passage you select (prepared as instructed on p. 73)

Procedure
Pairs of students play Rock, Paper, Scissors. To play game, students use these signs: rock—fist, paper—flat hand, scissors—cutting motion with index and middle fingers. **Scissors defeat paper because scissors cut paper. Paper defeats rock because paper covers rock. Rock defeats scissors because rock crushes scissors.** Students secretly choose signs. Pairs say "Rock, paper, scissors" aloud in unison and show chosen sign.

After three rounds, all students who won two out of three rounds tell their answers to one of the Discussion Cards.

Instant Activities
Room March

Materials
☐ Bibles
☐ Discussion Cards for Bible passage you select (prepared as instructed on p. 73)
☐ children's music cassette/CD and player

Procedure
Students form two single-file lines. As you play music, students follow the leader of their line around the room. When you stop the music, students freeze. Without looking at the students, name an object in the room (bookshelf, pencil sharpener, etc.). The student from each line who is closest to that object reads and answers one of

the Discussion Cards. Repeat, changing leaders and naming different objects.

Seat Switch

Materials
- ☐ Bibles
- ☐ Discussion Cards for Bible passage you select (prepared as instructed on p. 73)
- ☐ chairs

Procedure
Students sit in chairs. Name a category and begin naming things in that category (pets—dog, cat, hamster; vegetables—broccoli, corn, carrot). As soon as students hear you name something not in that category, students switch seats. Last student to find a new seat reads and answers a Discussion Card.

☀ Telephone

Materials
- ☐ Bibles
- ☐ Discussion Cards for Bible passage you select (prepared as instructed on p. 73)

Procedure
Divide class into groups of no more than six to eight. Each group forms a circle. Read part of a Discussion Card aloud and whisper the question on the card to one student in each circle. Student passes the question to the next person by whispering it to him or her. The last person to receive the question in each circle says it aloud (clarify as needed). Volunteers answer the question on the card. Repeat with other cards as time permits, each time beginning with a different student in the circle.

Instant Activities
☀The Most

Materials
☐ Bibles
☐ Discussion Cards for Bible passage you select (prepared as instructed on p. 73)

Procedure
Students stand in groups of three or four. Invite a volunteer to read one of the Discussion Cards. In each group, student with the most letters in his or her last name answers question on card. Repeat as time permits, reading new cards, changing groups and using other categories such as fewest letters in name, nearest birthday, wearing the most green, etc.

Instant Activities
☀Thumbs Up/Thumbs Down

Materials
☐ Bibles
☐ Discussion Cards for Bible passage you select (prepared as instructed on p. 73)

Procedure
Read one of the Discussion Cards aloud; then count "One, two, three." On "three," all students make a thumbs-up or a thumbs-down motion with one hand. Without looking at students, call "Thumbs-up" or "Thumbs-down." Volunteer from students holding thumb in position called answers question from Discussion Card.

☀ Two Corners

Materials
☐ Bibles
☐ Discussion Cards for Bible passage you select (prepared as instructed on p. 73)

Procedure
Students stand in the center of the room. Call out two flavors of ice cream, pointing to opposite corners of the room as you say each flavor. Each student goes to the corner of the room that indicates the flavor of ice cream he or she would choose. Read one of the Discussion Cards. Volunteers from each corner tell other students their answers. Repeat activity with other choices (sports, breakfast foods, etc.) and other cards.

Walk Around

Materials
☐ Bibles
☐ Discussion Cards for Bible passage you select (prepared as instructed on p. 73)
☐ children's music cassette/CD and player

Procedure
Students walk around in a circle while you play music. When music stops, student standing closest to the door (or other designated place) reads and answers one of the Discussion Cards. Repeat as time permits.

Discussion Cards
Tips for Preparing Discussion Cards

1. Check out the Discussion Card topics listed in the table of contents. Read the Bible passages listed and choose one that fits your focus.

2. Photocopy onto card stock or construction paper the three pages of Discussion Cards that fit your chosen Bible passage.

3. Cut cards apart using paper cutter or scissors. (Optional: Laminate or cover pages with clear Contact paper before cutting apart.)

4. Store the cards in a card-file box.

5. Use the cards in games and discussion activities as directed in this book.

What do you know about how a shepherd cares for sheep? What do you learn about God from Psalm 23?

Psalm 23

What tough times does Psalm 23 talk about? How did the writer say God helped him in those tough times?

Psalm 23

In what ways does the writer of Psalm 23 describe God's help and comfort in verses 1-4? When have you experienced God's help and comfort in these ways?

Psalm 23

When you think about the hard situations described in Psalm 23, which descriptions of God's help are most appealing to you? Why?

Psalm 23

The writer of Psalm 23 describes a green pasture and quiet waters. What scene would you choose to describe times when God has comforted you?

Psalm 23

In Psalm 23:4-6, what do you think is the writer's attitude about the future?

Psalm 23

According to Psalm 23:4-6, what are some reasons to be confident about God's help in the future?

Psalm 23

Someone lied about you to your best friend. Now your friend is angry and doesn't want to talk with you. Tomorrow you are going to a party and your best friend will be there. What do you do?

Psalm 23

Which verse or verses in Psalm 23 might help you when you feel like giving up? Why?

Psalm 23

In one month your mom is marrying a man with three kids! One of the kids is your age and doesn't like you. You hate the idea of having to live with hese people, especially the kid your age. What do you do?

Psalm 23

The writer of Psalm 23 compared God to a shepherd taking care of sheep. If the writer lived today, what are some jobs he might have chosen to illustrate God's care for us?

Psalm 23

You really like in-line skating. You've read about a competition that you would like to try out for. But you're afraid you won't be good enough. What do you do?

Psalm 23

Most of your friends are going to a different school next year. You're afraid you won't have any friends.
What do you do?

Psalm 23

You have been having trouble with math at school. You want to take algebra next year, but you're afraid you won't be able to pass it.
What do you do?

Psalm 23

Your friends want to go to a movie your parents said you couldn't see. You don't really want to see the movie, but you know your friends will want you to go, too.
What do you do?

Psalm 23

Someday you would like to be a veterinarian, but right now you would just like to have a pet. Your parents say they can't afford one.
What do you do?

Psalm 23

Your friend's parents are getting a divorce. You hear your parents argue sometimes and it scares you. You are afraid your parents will get a divorce, too.
What do you do?

Psalm 23

One of your dad's friends is dying of cancer. Your friend's aunt has cancer, too. You're worried that one of your parents will get cancer and die.
What do you do?

Psalm 23

What words does the writer of Psalm 51:1 use to describe God? What ideas about God do you get from those words?

Psalm 51:1-4,10-12

In Psalm 51:10, what do you think might be different between the two requests ("a pure heart" and "a steadfast spirit")? What might be the same about them?

Psalm 51:1-4,10-12

What does the writer of Psalm 51 ask God to do in verses 1-4? Why? When are some times kids your age might want to say words like these to God?

Psalm 51:1-4,10-12

In Psalm 51:1-4, what words refer to wrong things a person has done? If you were explaining these verses to a younger child what words might you use instead?

Psalm 51:1-4,10-12

How does the writer of Psalm 51 ask God to help him in verses 10-12? Choose one request and tell why a person who sins needs that from God.

Psalm 51:1-4,10-12

How would you say Psalm 51:10, 11 or 12 in simpler words?

Psalm 51:1-4,10-12

Discussion Cards • Psalm 51:1-4, 10-12

Why do you think the writer of Psalm 51 said in verse 3 that "my sin is always before me"? What does he ask God to do to solve that problem?

Psalm 51:1-4,10-12

You had an assignment due on Friday that you put off doing until Thursday night. But on Thursday, when you went to the library to get the book you needed to complete the assignment, it was checked out. There's no way to do a good job on the assignment without that book. What do you do?

Psalm 51:1-4,10-12

What phrases in Psalm 51:1-4,10-12 give clues about whether or not the writer will repeat the same sins again? Why?

Psalm 51:1-4,10-12

You and your friends really like to play basketball and decide to try out for an all-star basketball team. Your friends are chosen for the team, but you aren't. You feel like there's nothing you're good at doing. What do you do?

Psalm 51:1-4,10-12

How does the writer of Psalm 51:2 describe God's forgiveness of sin?

Psalm 51:1-4,10-12

The kids you usually spend time with after school swear a lot. After a while, you get into the habit of swearing, too. You've tried to stop swearing, but you just can't seem to break the habit. What do you do?

Psalm 51:1-4,10-12

When you're at your best friend's house, he gets a phone call from another good friend inviting him to an overnight pizza party. Because you haven't been invited, you feel like your friends don't really like you. What do you do?

Psalm 51:1-4,10-12

You find some cans of spray paint in the garage. You know it's not right, but you decide to try out the spray paint on the fence of a nearby construction site. You don't think anyone will be there because it's Saturday. However, the security guard catches you and calls the police and your parents. What do you do?

Psalm 51:1-4,10-12

A kid at school is always making fun of you. You haven't said anything back to the kid, but you wish she would just disappear. At school one day, you hear she has been in a serious bike accident. You feel terrible! What do you do?

Psalm 51:1-4,10-12

At the store you see a T-shirt you really want, but you don't have enough money to buy it. You manage to steal the shirt by stuffing it under your sweatshirt. When your parents ask about the shirt, you tell them it's one a kid at school didn't want any more. You're glad you have the shirt, but now you feel that God is mad at you. What do you do?

Psalm 51:1-4,10-12

You really want to go with your friends to the mall. You ask your dad, but he says you can't go. So you ask your mom without telling her that your dad already said no. She agrees and you go to the mall. When you come home, your parents are upset and disappointed at your actions. What do you say? What do you do?

Psalm 51:1-4,10-12

You have to give in front of your class a speech about a book. You memorize your speech and practice it a lot. You feel really nervous about the speech and halfway through, you completely forget what comes next. You make up an ending and quickly sit down, sure that your teacher will give you a bad grade on the speech. What do you do?

Psalm 51:1-4,10-12

In Psalm 139:1-3, what words are used that mean the same as "know"? What are some specific things God knows about us?

Psalm 139:1-3,13-16

If Psalm 139:1-3,13-16 was everything you knew about God, how would you describe Him?

Psalm 139:1-3,13-16

You have been asked to design a bumper sticker that states a main idea from Psalm 139:1-3. What would your bumper sticker say?

Psalm 139:1-3,13-16

When you read about how well God knows us in Psalm 139:1-3,13-16, how do you feel?

Psalm 139:1-3,13-16

What are some reasons Psalm 139:13-16 might help kids your age trust God?

Psalm 139:1-3,13-16

According to Psalm 139:14, what should be our response when we think about how God has made us?

Psalm 139:1-3,13-16

In Psalm 139:13-16, what words or phrases describe the way in which God made us?

Psalm 139:1-3,13-16

Your science report is due tomorrow. You have one section left to finish. Now your friend wants you to go to the mall. You think your teacher won't notice if you rush through the last section. Then you'd have time to go to the mall. What do you say to your friend? What do you choose to do?

Psalm 139:1-3,13-16

According to Psalm 139:1-3,13-16, why do you think God is the best One to help us accomplish good things?

Psalm 139:1-3,13-16

Your mom made you stay home and baby-sit your little sister, even though you wanted to play basketball with your friends. Usually you think of fun things for your sister to do with you. But today you're mad at being stuck at home. What do you do?

Psalm 139:1-3,13-16

What might make a kid feel nervous or worried about using his or her abilities? What information in Psalm 139:1-3,13-16 gives you confidence in using your abilities?

Psalm 139:1-3,13-16

You've taken piano lessons for a long time, but now you'd rather take guitar lessons. You know your parents will be disappointed if you stop taking piano lessons. What do you say to them?

Psalm 139:1-3,13-16

Somebody else was chosen to be the baseball team captain. You've never missed practice in two years and you always try to do your best. You don't think it's fair that someone else was chosen captain. Now you feel like quitting the team to pay back the coach for not choosing you. What do you do?

Psalm 139:1-3,13-16

You really like painting when you get your stuff out and do it, but it never seems like you have enough time. One day you see a TV commercial showing a kid painting. You think about getting out your paint stuff, but the TV show looks interesting. What do you do?

Psalm 139:1-3,13-16

You have always liked puppets and had fun doing shows for your little brothers. Now a puppet team is starting at your church and you want to join. But your best friend thinks puppets are dumb. What do you decide?

Psalm 139:1-3,13-16

You really like gymnastics. You are proud of the things you have learned to do. But there are three practices a week. The practices are hard work and sometimes you don't feel like going. Some kids don't go to all of the practices. What do you decide to do?

Psalm 139:1-3,13-16

There is a kid in your class who is shy and doesn't have many friends. Some of the kids in your class make fun of the shy kid. You are good at making friends and want to help this kid. But you worry your friends will make fun of you, too. What do you say to the shy kid? What do you say to your friends?

Psalm 139:1-3,13-16

You are one of three kids in your class left in a spelling contest. If you win, you'll be in a contest in front of the whole school! You don't like to stand up in front of lots of people, so you feel like misspelling a word on purpose to lose the contest. What do you do?

Psalm 139:1-3,13-16

In Psalm 146:7-10, what different actions of God are described? What do you learn about God from these actions?

Psalm 146:7-10

How might the words in Psalm 146:7-10 be comforting to someone who is discouraged by big problems?

Psalm 146:7-10

What ways to treat other people are described in Psalm 146:7-10? What words would you use to describe someone who treated people in these ways?

Psalm 146:7-10

What kinds of situations are described in these verses? Why might a person facing one of the situations in Psalm 146:7-10 want to praise God?

Psalm 146:7-10

Psalm 146:7-10 describes some ways that God helps people in difficult situations. When have you known or heard of someone in a difficult situation? What could a kid your age do to help a person in that situation?

Psalm 146:7-10

What are some ways kids your age could show compassion to people like those described in Psalm 146:7-10?

Psalm 146:7-10

According to Psalm 146:9, God "sustains" orphans and widows. What does it mean to sustain someone? What are some ways that we could help sustain people who are alone?

Psalm 146:7-10

A group of kids are making fun of a developmentally disabled student by imitating his voice when they talk to you. What do you say?

Psalm 146:7-10

According to Psalm 146:9, God "watches over" people who are strangers or outsiders. How can we watch over others who are alone because they are different in some way(s)?

Psalm 146:7-10

A girl in a wheelchair has started coming to your class. One day after school you are in a hurry to get to your bus, but she is in your way. What do you do?

Psalm 146:7-10

When have you seen someone care for the kinds of people described in Psalm 146:7-10? What happened as a result?

Psalm 146:7-10

There is a blind lady who lives next door to the aunt you are visiting. You meet her standing at a busy street corner. You wonder if you should help her across the street. What do you say or do?

Psalm 146:7-10

A man with a walker has dropped his book near you. He is trying very carefully to pick it up. What do you say or do?

Psalm 146:7-10

A family in your apartment building has several children. One child has several serious disabilities. What could you offer to do?

Psalm 146:7-10

A kid in your class who lives near you has to walk home from school with a sister who has something wrong with her muscles. You walk home the same way, but you don't feel comfortable being around the sister. What could you say or do?

Psalm 146:7-10

Kids at your school ignore the boy with braces on his legs because he moves slowly. He sits next to you in class and you know he is fun to talk to and smart. How could you help your other friends get to know him?

Psalm 146:7-10

Your grandpa comes to visit during holidays. He likes to talk to you, but he can't hear you very well. What do you do or say?

Psalm 146:7-10

You're having a party with music, food and games for the kids on your block. There is a mentally disabled girl on your block. You know she loves music even though she can't play the games. How do you decide to treat her at the party?

Psalm 146:7-10

Proverbs 3:3 says that we should keep love and faithfulness close to us. What do you think is the difference between love and faithfulness? Why do you think they should be so important to us?

Proverbs 3:3-6

Proverbs 3:3,4 says that showing love and faithfulness will give us a good name, or reputation. Why do you think it is important to have a good name, or reputation, in God's sight? Who are some people you have heard of who have good reputations?

Proverbs 3:3-6

Proverbs 3:3-6 tells us to show love and faithfulness constantly. What can we do to remember to show God's love and faithfulness to others?

Proverbs 3:3-6

Following Proverbs 3:3,4, what can people do to develop good names, or reputations, for themselves?

Proverbs 3:3-6

What are some things you can do to obey Proverbs 3:3 by showing love or faithfulness to a friend? To a family member?

Proverbs 3:3-6

Proverbs 3:5,6 tells us that when we trust in God's Word, He will make our paths straight. What are some other ways to describe what happens if we trust in God's Word?

Proverbs 3:3-6

Proverbs 3:6 tells us to "acknowledge Him." What is one way to do that? How can someone acknowledge God "in all" their ways?

Proverbs 3:3-6

A boy in your class draws a mean picture of the teacher and passes it around during lunch. Everyone laughs at the picture. If you don't laugh at the picture too, your friends might think you're weird. What will you say?

Proverbs 3:3-6

Proverbs 3:5 tells us to "lean not on your own understanding." What are some ways that depending on our own knowledge can cause trouble? Who should we lean, or depend, on instead?

Proverbs 3:3-6

On the bus to school, a popular girl asks to borrow your homework paper. She says she left her homework at home and she doesn't want to get a bad grade. What do you say to her?

Proverbs 3:3-6

What are some ways kids can show they trust in God? What is one thing you can do this week to put into practice the good advice of Proverbs 3:3-6?

Proverbs 3:3-6

A boy at school always makes fun of you. You feel awful and wonder if anyone really likes you. What do you do?

Proverbs 3:3-6

You want to be the first one of your friends to buy the new CD by your favorite singer so that your friends will really like you. But your dad says you can't have the money to buy it. What do you say to your dad?

Proverbs 3:3-6

You've never gotten anything less than an A on your report card. Now your teacher assigns you to work on a science-fair project with a kid who never gets work done on time. What do you do?

Proverbs 3:3-6

After school today, you are planning to try out for an all-star basketball team. A kid you know who is a good player asks when the tryouts are. You don't want to tell him because he might be chosen for the team instead of you. What do you say to him?

Proverbs 3:3-6

Your family has just moved to a new town. A lot of your old friends went to church with you. But in your new neighborhood, all the kids you've just made friends with don't go to church. What do you say when they want to play with you on Sunday morning?

Proverbs 3:3-6

Your friends spend a lot of money at the mall. You don't have as much money as they do, but your parents promised to raise your allowance. Now, however, they can't afford to give more money. What do you do when you're at the mall with your friends?

Proverbs 3:3-6

Your parents won't let you watch the movies most of your friends get to see. You're afraid your friends will stop inviting you to their parties. What do you say to one of your friends when she asks you to come over to watch a movie?

Proverbs 3:3-6

Seven times in Matthew 5:3-9 Jesus uses the word "blessed." What does it mean for someone to be blessed? What are some other words that communicate a similar idea?

Matthew 5:3-9

Read Matther 5:6. What might a person who hungers and thirsts after righteousness, or goodness, do?

Matthew 5:3-9

According to Matthew 5:5, Jesus says that meek, or humble, people will inherit the earth. What do you think that means?

Matthew 5:3-9

In Matthew 5:7, Jesus talked about showing mercy. What's so great about being shown mercy? How can you show mercy to others?

Matthew 5:3-9

Read Mathew 5:5. Who do you know that is humble? Why do you think this person is humble? How can kids your age show meekness?

Matthew 5:3-9

Read Matthew 5:8. How many different ways can you think of to say that someone is sincere, or pure in heart?

Matthew 5:3-9

Which of the actions or attitudes described in Matthew 5:3-9 is the easiest for you to do or have? the hardest? Why?

Matthew 5:3-9

Two of your friends are arguing about which music group is the best. Each one wants you to be on his or her side. What do you decide to do?

Matthew 5:3-9

Of all the good results Jesus talked about in Matthew 5:3-9, which one sounds best to you? Why?

Matthew 5:3-9

Your friend tells you a story that you know is a lie about one of your friends. What do you say?

Matthew 5:3-9

Of all the different kinds of people Jesus mentioned in Matthew 5:3-9, which ones would be most likely to make your school better? Your neighborhood? Your family?

Matthew 5:3-9

A friend of yours is afraid of failing a test and getting in trouble at home. He says the only way to stay out of trouble is to copy your answers. What do you decide to say and do?

Matthew 5:3-9

Some of your friends decide it would be funny for each kid to steal a piece of candy from a store. If you don't join them, you're afraid they won't hang out with you anymore. What do you do?

Matthew 5:3-9 _____

Your little brother knows just how to get on your nerves. And he's always whining about something. Now he's whining that he wants you to play with him—again. What do you say and do?

Matthew 5:3-9

One of your friends at church likes to make fun of another kid in your class so that everyone else laughs. What can you do or say?

Matthew 5:3-9 _____

Your friend is sad because she wasn't chosen to play on a club soccer team. But you are excited because you were not only chosen to play on the team, but you're also a starter. What can you say to your friend?

Matthew 5:3-9 _____

You know that you should ask before borrowing things. But your sister ALWAYS borrows your things without asking. She's not home and you want to use her bike. What do you do?

Matthew 5:3-9 _____

Your older brother won an art award. Everyone is bragging about him. You don't think you have any talent where art is concerned. What do you do?

Matthew 5:3-9

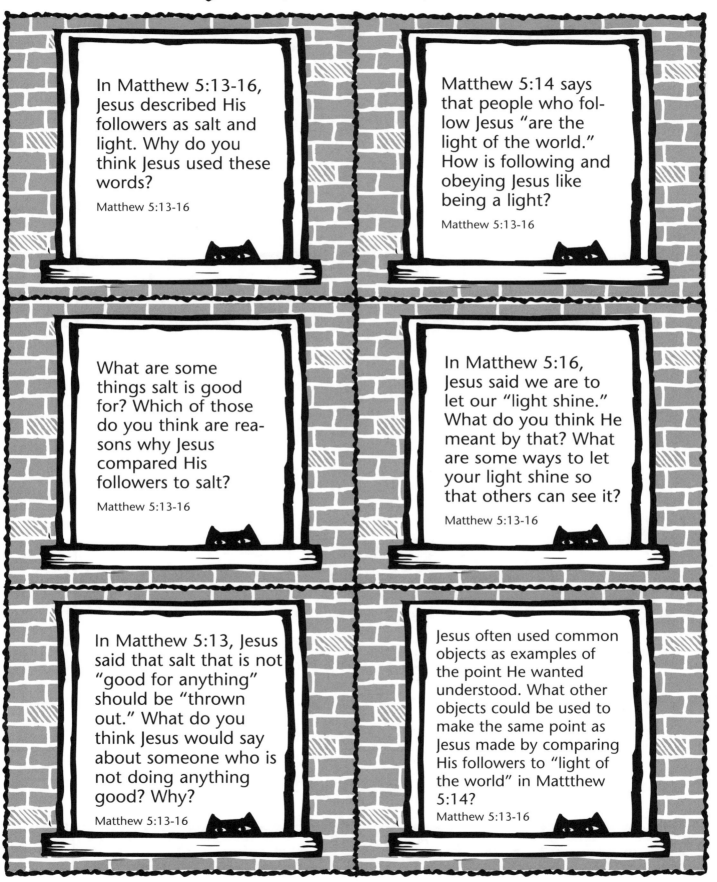

In Matthew 5:13-16, Jesus described His followers as salt and light. Why do you think Jesus used these words?

Matthew 5:13-16

Matthew 5:14 says that people who follow Jesus "are the light of the world." How is following and obeying Jesus like being a light?

Matthew 5:13-16

What are some things salt is good for? Which of those do you think are reasons why Jesus compared His followers to salt?

Matthew 5:13-16

In Matthew 5:16, Jesus said we are to let our "light shine." What do you think He meant by that? What are some ways to let your light shine so that others can see it?

Matthew 5:13-16

In Matthew 5:13, Jesus said that salt that is not "good for anything" should be "thrown out." What do you think Jesus would say about someone who is not doing anything good? Why?

Matthew 5:13-16

Jesus often used common objects as examples of the point He wanted understood. What other objects could be used to make the same point as Jesus made by comparing His followers to "light of the world" in Mattthew 5:14?

Matthew 5:13-16

Jesus said that a light is put on a stand in a house, so everyone in the house can see the light. How can you be a light and show God's love in your home? Where else can you be a light by showing God's love?

Matthew 5:13-16

On your way to the bus stop you see a younger kid who is crying. What do you do?

Matthew 5:13-16

Matthew 5:16 tells us to let our lights shine so that others can praise God. Why do you think praising God is important?

Matthew 5:13-16

The old man who lives next door to you tells you and your dad about his son who can't come home to see him. What can you say and do?

Matthew 5:13-16

According to Matthew 5:14-16, what are some good deeds that can cause people to praise God?

Matthew 5:13-16

One of your friends is from another country. He speaks English pretty well, but his little sister is having a hard time in school. She can't understand what the teacher says. What can you say or do?

Matthew 5:13-16

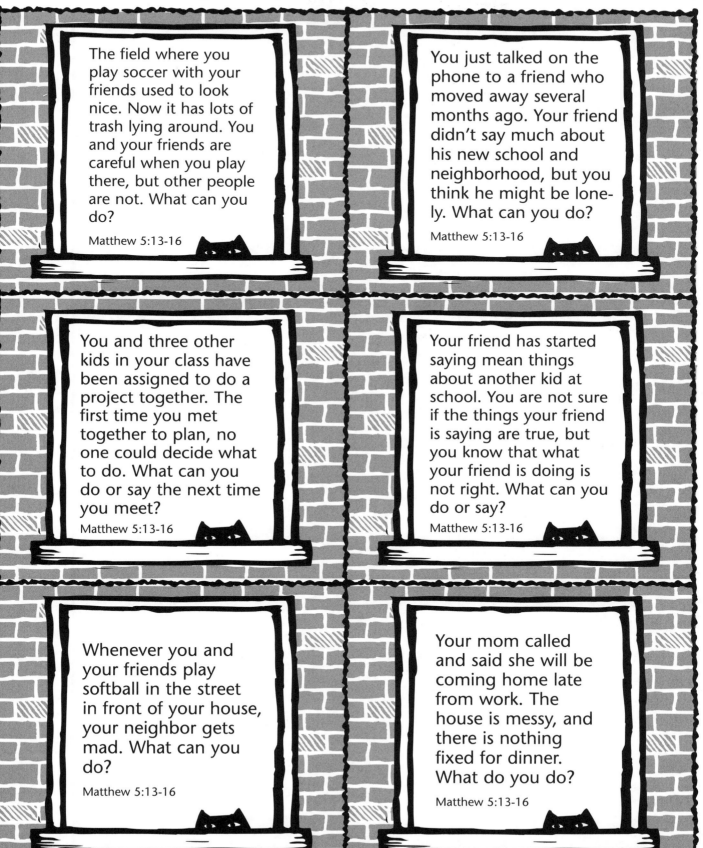

The field where you play soccer with your friends used to look nice. Now it has lots of trash lying around. You and your friends are careful when you play there, but other people are not. What can you do?

Matthew 5:13-16

You just talked on the phone to a friend who moved away several months ago. Your friend didn't say much about his new school and neighborhood, but you think he might be lonely. What can you do?

Matthew 5:13-16

You and three other kids in your class have been assigned to do a project together. The first time you met together to plan, no one could decide what to do. What can you do or say the next time you meet?

Matthew 5:13-16

Your friend has started saying mean things about another kid at school. You are not sure if the things your friend is saying are true, but you know that what your friend is doing is not right. What can you do or say?

Matthew 5:13-16

Whenever you and your friends play softball in the street in front of your house, your neighbor gets mad. What can you do?

Matthew 5:13-16

Your mom called and said she will be coming home late from work. The house is messy, and there is nothing fixed for dinner. What do you do?

Matthew 5:13-16

In Matthew 6:9-13, Jesus taught His disciples how to pray. What have you learned from other people about how to pray?

Matthew 6:9-13

In Matthew 6:9, Jesus said to pray that the name of God will be "hallowed," or treated with great respect and honor. What are some ways people treat God's name disrespect-fully? Respectfully?

Matthew 6:9-13

In Matthew 6:9-13, what are some things Jesus said we should pray about? When might be a good time to pray "hallowed be your name" or one of the other phrases in the verses?

Matthew 6:9-13

In Matthew 6:10, Jesus prayed for something so important that He asked for it twice, saying the same thing in two ways. What do you think He wants to happen when He says that, "your kingdom come, your will be done"?

Matthew 6:9-13

In Matthew 6:9, what name did Jesus call God? How is God like a father?

Matthew 6:9-13

In Matthew 6:11, why do you think Jesus said to pray, "Give us today our daily bread"? Besides food, what are some things we need every day that might be included in this request?

Matthew 6:9-13

In Matthew 6:12, why do you think that when Jesus talked about asking God to forgive us, He also talked about us forgiving others?

Matthew 6:9-13

You told your mom you thought a boy at church was cute. Your mom told his mom and really embarrassed you. You yelled at your mom because she told your secret, but now you're sorry for the things you said. What can you say to your mom?

Matthew 6:9-13

When might be a good time to say something like Matthew 6:13 as a prayer? What are some common temptations kids face?

Matthew 6:9-13

You laughed at your best friend the other day, and now she is really mad. You're sorry you hurt her feelings. What can you do to be friends again?

Matthew 6:9-13

What practical steps can kids your age take to stay away from temptations to do wrong things?

Matthew 6:9-13

You decided to get your brother back for spying on you and your friends. You said some really mean things about him to your friends when you knew he was listening. After your friends went home, you saw your brother crying. What can you do?

Matthew 6:9-13

You were watching TV when you should have been doing your homework. Your dad came in, turned off the TV and started yelling about your grades at school. You were going to do your homework as soon as the show was over, but he wouldn't even listen. Now he won't let you watch TV all weekend. What can you say to your dad? What can you say to God?

Matthew 6:9-13

You and several of your friends were sitting on the window ledge at school during lunch. While you were fooling around, one of your friends pushed you and you fell backwards, accidentally breaking the window. You didn't get hurt, but now you need to tell a teacher about the broken window. What do you say to the teacher?

Matthew 6:9-13

You saw that your dad left some money out on his desk. Without really thinking about it, you took some of it. Later you hear your dad asking your brother and sister if they took the money. You know he's going to ask you, too. What do you say?

Matthew 6:9-13

Instead of writing your own story for a class assignment, you decide to copy a story from a children's magazine. Several weeks later, your teacher tells you that because the story was so well written, she has entered it in a city-wide story contest. What can you do?

Matthew 6:9-13

You were clowning around with some of your friends after church last week. There was a poster of dinosaurs on the wall. Your friend drew funny pictures on the poster. Pretty soon you were all drawing on it. Now the teacher in that room is really upset. She wants to know who ruined her poster. What can you do?

Matthew 6:9-13

You borrowed your best friend's new CD. You left it on the floor in your room and your little brother stepped on it and broke it. You were so mad, you hit your brother! Now your parents are mad at you for hitting him. And you know your friend will be mad at you, too. What can you do and say?

Matthew 6:9-13

What are some things that people value or treasure? What do kids your age value a lot? What does Matthew 6:19 say about these kinds of treasures?

Matthew 6:19-21,24

Read Matthew 6:19,20. What are some ways that people get "treasures on earth"? How do you think we store up "treasures in heaven"?

Matthew 6:19-21,24

What are some differences between "treasures on earth" and "treasures in heaven" as talked about in Matthew 6:19,20?

Matthew 6:19-21,24

Read Matthew 6:19,20. How can your actions show that you want to store up "treasures in heaven"?

Matthew 6:19-21,24

Matthew 6:19 tells us not to treasure, or value, things that thieves can "break in and steal." What kinds of things can't be stolen from us?

Matthew 6:19-21,24

What do you think Jesus meant in Matthew 6:21 when He said, "For where your treasure is, there your heart will be also"?

Matthew 6:19-21,24

Matthew 6:24 says that we can't be devoted to God and to money at the same time. What does it mean to be devoted to something? How do people act if they are devoted to money? How can you show that you are devoted to God?

Matthew 6:19-21,24

Your baseball team isn't very good. Most of the players can't hit or field very well. You used to be on a team that won all the time. Your new team never wins. Some of the people from your old team have started making fun of you. What can you do or say?

Matthew 6:19-21,24

Why does Matthew 6:24 say that people cannot serve both God and money?

Matthew 6:19-21,24

Your friends all have in-line skates and street-hockey gear. Your family can't afford to buy the same stuff for you. You are scared that you will lose your friends since you can't play hockey with them. What will you do?

Matthew 6:19-21,24

Why do you think Matthew 6:24 calls money a master? What are some other things that sometimes seem to take over people's lives?

Matthew 6:19-21,24

There was a fire that destroyed the house of a kid in your class. All the kid's clothes, toys and other stuff was burned up. You have plenty of clothes, but you really like all of them. What will you do?

Matthew 6:19-21,24

You are really good at math. Another kid in your math class is having a hard time. She rides the same bus you do, and you sat with her to explain the math assignment on the way home. But your best friend got mad because you didn't sit with her. What do you do?

Matthew 6:19-21,24

Your friend wants you to spend the night at his house. Your friend's family doesn't go to church and the last time you spent the night there you were too tired to get up and go to church the next morning. What will you do?

Matthew 6:19-21,24

One of your friends invited you to a party but told you that another one of your friends wasn't invited because no one likes her. You don't think it is right to be mean to her. What do you do?

Matthew 6:19-21,24

On Saturday morning, your parents ask you to clean the house before you spend time with your friends. You know you can get away with doing a sloppy job. What will you do?

Matthew 6:19-21,24

Your soccer team is playing for the championship. Your team needs to play its best to win. Your foot is hurt, but you still want to play. Another kid on the team is as good as you and would be able to play if you didn't. When your coach asks how your foot feels, what will you say?

Matthew 6:19-21,24

Your big sister is in trouble with your parents because they think she scratched the car when she borrowed it to drive to the mall. Your sister says she didn't do it. No one knows that you hit the car with your bike after she got home. What will you do?

Matthew 6:19-21,24

Discussion Cards • Romans 8:35,37-39

When might kids your age feel that God doesn't love them? Why? What does Romans 8:35,37 say that could help someone who doesn't feel loved by God?

Romans 8:35,37-39

Romans 8:38,39 lists things that cannot separate us from God's love or cause God to stop loving us. What specific situations could you add to that list?

Romans 8:35,37-39

Paul faced all the troubles listed in Romans 8:35. Which of these troubles sounds most difficult to you? How do you think God might help someone in one of these situations?

Romans 8:35,37-39

What are some things in the present that might worry kids your age? In the future? What does Romans 8:38,39 promise us?

Romans 8:35,37-39

What does Romans 8:37 say we are when we face big problems? How are we able to conquer such terrible problems?

Romans 8:35,37-39

Choose one of the situations in Romans 8:35. How can God help someone who is in this situation?

Romans 8:35,37-39

Discussion Cards • Romans 8:35,37-39

In Romans 8:38,39, Paul says that he is convinced that nothing could separate him from God's love. What do you think gave Paul confidence in God's love for him?

Romans 8:35,37-39

Your friend is really afraid of having to give an oral book report in class. What do you say to give encouragement?

Romans 8:35,37-39

What words from Romans 8:35,37-39 would encourage you most if you were in a fearful situation?

Romans 8:35,37-39

Your friend thinks he won't get a good grade on a math test. He is afraid his mom will be mad at him. What can you do?

Romans 8:35,37-39

Romans 8:39 says that nothing can separate us from God's love. When are some times that knowing about God's love would be encouraging?

Romans 8:35,37-39

The kid who lives down the street from you is at the baseball team tryouts alone and looks nervous. You are there with both your parents. What do you do?

Romans 8:35,37-39

When baby-sitting your little sister who's afraid of the dark, what do you do at her bedtime?

Romans 8:35,37-39

The boy next door has to move and is afraid he won't make new friends. What can you do and say?

Romans 8:35,37-39

Your friend has nightmares of being in a fire. What can you say and do?

Romans 8:35,37-39

Your friend was beaten up by some kids once this year and is afraid it will happen again. What do you do?

Romans 8:35,37-39

Your friend doesn't let other kids know that she is a Christian because she is afraid they will think she's weird. What can you say and do?

Romans 8:35,37-39

On the way to school, your little brother is afraid of walking past the yard with the big gray dog. What can you say to him? What can you do?

Romans 8:35,37-39

Imagine that our class was being graded on how well we obey Romans 12:9,10. What grade do you think we would get? What are some actions that might raise our grade? Lower our grade?

Romans 12:9-14,17-21

How can your words show that you care about others' needs and interests? How can your words demonstrate hospitality or generosity? How can your actions show these things?

Romans 12:9-14,17-21

Which of the instructions in Romans 12:9-14 do you think would help kids your age the most in showing God's love to other kids at school? Why?

Romans 12:9-14,17-21

When are some times kids your age feel persecuted or mistreated? How can kids your age obey Romans 12:14 and do good to the people who mistreat them in situations like these?

Romans 12:9-14,17-21

What is one way you could obey the instructions in Romans 12:10 when you have a disagreement with a friend?

Romans 12:9-14,17-21

What difference would it make in your school or your neighborhood if kids followed the instructions in Romans 12:17?

Romans 12:9-14,17-21

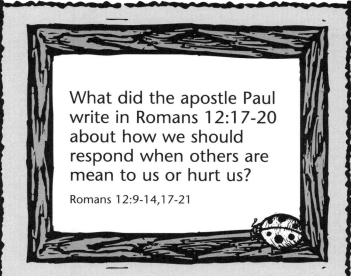

What did the apostle Paul write in Romans 12:17-20 about how we should respond when others are mean to us or hurt us?

Romans 12:9-14, 17-21

You are angry with your friend for something she said. Your friend knows that you are upset but doesn't apologize. Now you're trying to decide whether or not to invite your friend to your birthday party. What do you do?

Romans 12:9-14, 17-21

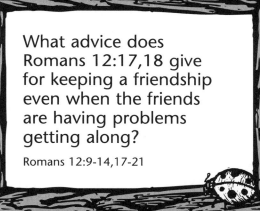

What advice does Romans 12:17,18 give for keeping a friendship even when the friends are having problems getting along?

Romans 12:9-14, 17-21

Your best friend found out that you told something that was supposed to be a secret. What can you say and do?

Romans 12:9-14, 17-21

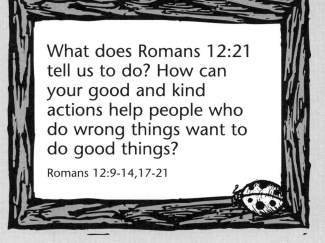

What does Romans 12:21 tell us to do? How can your good and kind actions help people who do wrong things want to do good things?

Romans 12:9-14, 17-21

Your friend borrowed your favorite CD. Now it has scratches on it and won't play. You think your friend should pay for a new CD. Your friend said the scratches were there already. What do you do?

Romans 12:9-14, 17-21

You helped with your friend's science project. Your friend won the science fair and got two tickets to an amusement park. Your friend invited another kid from your class instead of you. What do you say to your friend?

Romans 12:9-14,17-21

Your friend goes to a new school now and is making new friends. Whenever you call your friend on the phone, your friend is busy. What do you do to keep your friend even when you can't spend much time together?

Romans 12:9-14,17-21

Your friend just got moved to an advanced English class. The teacher said that your grades were not good enough to get into that class. You're worried your friend will think you're dumb. What do you do to keep on being a friend?

Romans 12:9-14,17-21

You and your friend sometimes watch a little kid's television program and laugh about it. Your friend told some other kids that you still watch that program, and the other kids start making fun of you. What do you say the next time you talk to your friend?

Romans 12:9-14,17-21

Your friend has started spending time with a new kid who has a lot of cool stuff. When the three of you are together, you feel left out. They invited you to go to the mall with them, but you'd rather do something with just your friend. What do you say?

Romans 12:9-14,17-21

You and your friend are camping in your backyard. Somehow when you were trying to set up your dad's lantern, it broke. Now your dad is mad. When he asks what happened, what do you say?

Romans 12:9-14,17-21

Which actions described in 1 Corinthians 13:4-8a could you do to help the people you live with? What might happen as a result of your actions?

1 Corinthians 13:4-8a

According to 1 Corinthians 13:5, what is the love God wants us to have not like? When is it hard not to have these attitudes?

1 Corinthians 13:4-8a

How did Jesus demonstrate the kind of love described in 1 Corinthians 13:4-8a?

1 Corinthians 13:4-8a

1 Corinthians 13:6 says love "rejoices with the truth." How is being truthful a way to show love? How does not rejoicing in evil show the way God wants us to love?

1 Corinthians 13:4-8a

How could you show the kind of love described in 1 Corinthians 13:4 to a friend? To someone who is not a friend?

1 Corinthians 13:4-8a

1 Corinthians 13:7 lists four ways God wants us to love others. What is a way a kid your age can show love to a friend in these ways?

1 Corinthians 13:4-8a

What might happen if you choose to do some of the actions described in 1 Corinthians 13:4-8a when you feel angry? How do you think your attitude might change? How might the attitudes of people around you change?

1 Corinthians 13:4-8a

Your mom gave you some clothes you really don't want to wear. She wants to know why you haven't been wearing the clothes she gave you. What do you say?

1 Corinthians 13:4-8a

When have you seen someone show God's love in one or more of the ways described in 1 Corinthians 13:4-8a?

1 Corinthians 13:4-8a

Your aunt gave your little brother some money for his birthday. He lost it in the bedroom you both share, and he's blaming you! What do you say to your brother?

1 Corinthians 13:4-8a

---

1 Corinthians 13:4-8a describes God's love. What is one specific way you can show God's love to another person today?

1 Corinthians 13:4-8a

Your sister and you always fight about who gets to use the bathroom first in the morning. What can you and your sister do to stop your arguments?

1 Corinthians 13:4-8a

Discussion Cards • 1 Corinthians 13:4-8a

Your little brother is always following you around. He wants to do everything that you do. You want to spend some time alone with your friends. What do you say to your brother?

1 Corinthians 13:4-8a

Your dad is upset because your grades are too low. You know you've been doing your best, but your dad doesn't seem to believe you. You feel that your dad isn't being fair. What do you say?

1 Corinthians 13:4-8a

Your grandmother is coming to live with your family. Your mom says that the best room for her to stay in is yours, since it is next to the bathroom and she wouldn't have to climb any stairs. You love your grandmother, but you don't want to give up your room. What do you do and say?

1 Corinthians 13:4-8a

You live with your mom and visit your dad on the weekends. Your dad just got a job in another state. Now you won't be able to visit him as often. You are afraid that your dad will forget about you. What do you do?

1 Corinthians 13:4-8a

Your mom is in the hospital. You want to go and see her every day after school, but your dad doesn't get home from work in time to take you. What can you do to show love to your mom?

1 Corinthians 13:4-8a

Your sister said some mean things about you that really hurt your feelings. What can you say to your sister?

1 Corinthians 13:4-8a

Galatians 5:22,23 lists nine character traits, or ways of acting, that God's Spirit helps us develop. When have you seen someone show one of these character traits?

Galatians 5:22,23

What can a person do to develop the characteristics listed in Galatians 5:22,23?

Galatians 5:22,23

Read Galatians 5:22. What might remind you to show love? Joy? Peace?

Galatians 5:22,23

What do you think the last part of Galatians 5:23 means? Why would there be no law against showing the fruit of the Spirit?

Galatians 5:22,23

Think of a time you have seen someone demonstrate some of the characteristics listed in Galatians 5:22,23. What happened because the person acted in that way?

Galatians 5:22,23

What does fruit need to grow? Why do you think the character traits in Galatians 5:22,23 are referred to as fruit? What can help you grow this spiritual fruit?

Galatians 5:22,23

Read Galatians 5:22,23 and choose one characteristic. What might happen in your family if you demonstrated that characteristic?

Galatians 5:22,23

Your brother wore your favorite sweatshirt to play mud football. He washed it, but the stains didn't come out. You feel mad, but what do you do to keep the peace?

Galatians 5:22,23

Which of the characteristics in Galatians 5:22,23 do you think kids in your class at school need to show? Why?

Galatians 5:22,23

You have a big project due Friday and a big soccer game on Saturday. You need to practice for the game, but you also need to spend time on your project. How can you show goodness and do both of these things?

Galatians 5:22,23

What is the easiest character trait listed in Galatians 5:22,23 for you to show? Which is the hardest? What can you do when you need help showing this character trait?

Galatians 5:22,23

Even though you have a lot of homework and chores to do, what good things has God given you that can help you be joyful?

Galatians 5:22,23

Your mother told you to help take care of your little sister for the afternoon, but you wanted to go to your friend's house to play video games. What can you do to show kindness?

Galatians 5:22,23

You promised to spend the afternoon with a friend, but now a really popular kid wants you to go to the mall with her. What do you do? Why?

Galatians 5:22,23

Your little brother is annoying you and your friends. What can you say or do to treat your brother gently and kindly?

Galatians 5:22,23

Your friend is having a hard time doing the math homework. You patiently tried to explain how to do the math problems, but your friend doesn't understand and wants you to explain again. What do you do?

Galatians 5:22,23

There is a kid in your class who most of the other kids make fun of. You don't think it is fair to treat him this way. What good thing can you do to show God's love to him?

Galatians 5:22,23

When your friends make fun of the substitute teacher and cause problems, what can you do to show self-control?

Galatians 5:22,23

Paul, one of Jesus' followers, wrote Ephesians 4:1-6 to describe God's plan for the people who believe in Him. What do you think is the most important instruction that Paul wrote in Ephesians 4:1-3 for the Church family?

Ephesians 4:1-6

How many different ways can you think of to say what Ephesians 4:3 tells us to make every effort to do? What does it mean to "keep the unity" with other Christians?

Ephesians 4:1-6

Ephesians 4:2,3 tells us good ways to treat each other. Which do you think is hardest for most people to do? Why?

Ephesians 4:1-6

Read Ephesians 4:3. Why do you think people who follow Jesus need to have unity or work together?

Ephesians 4:1-6

What are some examples of ways we can obey the instructions in Ephesians 4:2?

Ephesians 4:1-6

In Ephesians 4:4, Paul used the word "body" to describe the Church, or the group of people who follow Jesus. How is a church like a body?

Ephesians 4:1-6

In Ephesians 4:4-6, why do you think Paul keeps emphasizing the word "one"? Why do you think it is important that there is only one of each of the things mentioned in these verses?

Ephesians 4:1-6

You're on your way to your class at church and you see some parents with a baby. The mother asks you where the nursery is. What do you do?

Ephesians 4:1-6

What does Ephesians 4:6 tell us about God? How might knowing this help God's followers work together?

Ephesians 4:1-6

You and your best friend walk into your class at church. The teacher isn't there yet, but a new kid and his dad are in the room. What do you say?

Ephesians 4:1-6

If two groups of Christians disagree with each other, how could Ephesians 4:3-6 help them keep from arguing and getting mad?

Ephesians 4:1-6

One of the kids in your class at church bumps into you and knocks you down while you are doing a relay. How do you act?

Ephesians 4:1-6

One of your friends starts a water fight in the bathroom at church. You know that playing this way will make a big mess. What do you do?

Ephesians 4:1-6

In the church parking lot, you notice a little kid you've never seen before who is crying. What do you say? What do you do?

Ephesians 4:1-6

Your church collects gifts for needy families. What kinds of things do you decide to give?

Ephesians 4:1-6

You and your friends see a teacher carrying several boxes of supplies to his classroom. What do you say and do?

Ephesians 4:1-6

Your class has a picnic at a local park. The group before you left the picnic site a little messy. What do you do?

Ephesians 4:1-6

You have two little brothers. Your mom has a hard time getting them ready for church in the morning. What can you say and do?

Ephesians 4:1-6

If everyone followed the instructions of Ephesians 4:29, what change would you notice in your favorite TV show? Your friends at school? Your family? Yourself?

Ephesians 4:29—5:1

What advice does Ephesians 4:29—5:1 give us about how to treat others when we're angry or when someone is angry with us?

Ephesians 4:29—5:1

Ephesians 4:29 tells us not to let "unwholesome talk come out of [our] mouths." How would getting rid of "unwholesome talk" help stop some of the behaviors mentioned in verse 31?

Ephesians 4:29—5:1

How would you say Ephesians 4:31 in your own words?

Ephesians 4:29—5:1

Ephesians 4:29 tells us we should say things that "build others up." What good things can happen when we use kind and encouraging words? What are some examples of words that "build others up"?

Ephesians 4:29—5:1

The word "slander" in Ephesians 4:31 means unkind lies that hurt a person's feelings and reputation. What can you do when you feel like saying unkind things about other people?

Ephesians 4:29—5:1

Ephesians 4:32 says we should forgive others just as Jesus has forgiven us. What happens when someone refuses to forgive another person?

Ephesians 4:29—5:1

You got home from school before your brother and borrowed a computer game from his room. But when he came home, he yelled at you when he saw you playing it. What do you say to your brother?

Ephesians 4:29—5:1

Ephesians 5:1 says that we should imitate God "as dearly loved children" imitate their parents. How can knowing that we are loved dearly by God help us follow the instructions in Ephesians 4:29-32?

Ephesians 4:29—5:1

Your best friend told another friend that you liked someone you really don't like. What do you say to your best friend?

Ephesians 4:29—5:1

How would you sum up the ways Ephesians 4:29—5:1 tells members of God's family to imitate God? When can you follow these instructions?

Ephesians 4:29—5:1

While several friends are at your house, your mom asks you to do a chore you forgot to do. What do you say to her?

Ephesians 4:29—5:1

Discussion Cards • Ephesians 4:29-5:1

A kid on your soccer team accidentally scores a goal for the other team. Everyone on your team is mad! What do you say to the kid who made the mistake?

Ephesians 4:29—5:1

People usually laugh at your jokes. But today, your friend got mad at you when you said something funny about her. You know you hurt her feelings. What do you say to her?

Ephesians 4:29—5:1

Your friends tell mean jokes. You don't like their jokes. What do you say to your friends?

Ephesians 4:29—5:1

Your neighbor is mean to the kids in the neighborhood. He yells at you and your friends for sitting on the curb by his house. What do you say to your friends about him?

Ephesians 4:29—5:1

You and your best friend ride to school in the same carpool. Yesterday you and your friend had a big argument. Today, when you get in the car, your friend doesn't even look at you. What do you say?

Ephesians 4:29—5:1

You've been wanting to go to the new amusement park. Your friend asked another friend to go with him instead of you. What do you say to your friend?

Ephesians 4:29—5:1

What are some instructions you know from God's Word? What does James 1:22 tell us to do since we know these instructions from God's Word?

James 1:22-25

James 1:25 says that a person should read and study God's Word intently. What do you think that means? When can you study God's Word?

James 1:22-25

James 1:22 says that if we listen to God's Word without also obeying it, we can deceive ourselves. How does obeying the Word keep us from deceiving ourselves?

James 1:22-25

What are some ways that paying attention to and obeying God's Word can bless or help us as promised in James 1:25?

James 1:22-25

Why does James 1:23 describe God's Word as a mirror?

James 1:22-25

What does James 1:22 tell us to do? How can we remind ourselves to study God's Word and obey it?

James 1:22-25

Read James 1:22. What are some ways you can show that you listen to and obey God's Word?

James 1:22-25

You've always been told not to steal, but your friend shows you a way to bang on a vending machine to get a free soda. You think that a soda is such a small item, it won't really matter if you take just one for free. What do you say to your friend? What do you do?

James 1:22-25

What does James 1:22-25 say are ways to show you value God's Word?

James 1:22-25

Your teacher gives you a note about your low math grades to give to your parents. You make plans to study harder and ask the teacher for extra help. But then you wonder if you really have to give the note to your parents. You're afraid they'll be upset with you. What do you do?

James 1:22-25

Read James 1:22-25. When are some times it is hard to remember and obey God's Word? What can you do when you don't feel like obeying God's Word?

James 1:22-25

Your grandma comes to live at your house. You love your grandma a lot. But when your friends come over to play computer games, you feel embarrassed by the funny clothes your grandma wears. What do you say to your friends? How do you treat your grandma?

James 1:22-25

The teacher asked you to work with a new kid on a class project. Even though you didn't really want to work with someone new, you did and became friends with the new kid. But at school, your other friends ignore the new kid. What do you do and say to your friends?

James 1:22-25

You are home after school by yourself. A friend asks if he can come over. You call your dad at the office, and he says it's OK. When your friend comes, however, he brings a video you know you're not allowed to watch. What do you do?

James 1:22-25

You are chosen as the captain of your school's basketball team. One kid on the team is the worst player in the school. The rules say you have to let everyone play the same amount of time, but you know the teachers are too busy to make sure the rules are followed. What do you do?

James 1:22-25

You belong to a mail-order computer game club. The club sends you an extra computer game that you didn't order. You think they will send you a bill for the game, but they never do. What do you do?

James 1:22-25

On your way out of school, you notice a twenty-dollar bill on the walkway. You look around but don't see anyone who looks like they've lost money. You even wait for a few minutes to see if anyone comes back for the money. When no one comes, you wonder if it's OK to keep the money for yourself. What do you do?

James 1:22-25

You always turn in your school reports on on time, but you just remembered that your social studies report is due the next day. While you are looking on your family's bookshelf for a reference book, you find your older brother's report. You think about copying his report. What do you do?

James 1:22-25

How does 1 John 3:16 describe God's love? How did Jesus lay down His life? How can we "lay down our lives" to show love to others?

1 John 3:16-18

What situation is described in 1 John 3:17? Why do you think it is important to not just claim to love other people but also show love with our actions?

1 John 3:16-18

What example does 1 John 3:17 give as a way to show God's love? What are some other ways to show God's love?

1 John 3:16-18

Based on 1 John 3:16-18, how would you define what it means to truly show God's love to someone?

1 John 3:16-18

How can you show the kind of love described in 1 John 3:16-18 to a person who feels lonely? Who is sick? Who needs to know about Jesus?

1 John 3:16-18

What does 1 John 3:17 tell us to do with our material possessions? What are some things that you can share with others? Who do you know who might need something you could share?

1 John 3:16-18

1 John 3:16-18 says we should show love to others. How can you show this love to people at school? At home? At church?

1 John 3:16-18

A boy at camp got caught stealing money from another camper. Everyone is now avoiding the boy, calling him names. What should you do?

1 John 3:16-18

When have people in your family shown love to you? What actions did they do to show love? What words did they use?

1 John 3:16-18

A new girl at school wears clothes that only younger kids wear. Your friends make fun of her. Why might the new girl not dress like everyone else? What could you say to your friends?

1 John 3:16-18

Sometimes it is easier to say kind words than to take time to help someone with a problem. What does 1 John 3:18 say is the right way to show love? Why do you think actions are more important than words?

1 John 3:16-18

Your friends wanted another friend to buy a particular CD with his gift certificate. Your friend said he wouldn't because the music tells people to do wrong things. Now your friends say he is weird. What do you do?

1 John 3:16-18

You and your friends are trying to decide which video to rent. One friend's parents won't let her watch R-rated movies, so your friends want to watch a movie without her. What do you think? What will you do?

1 John 3:16-18

Your baseball team had a chance to tie the game; but the last kid up to bat struck out and your team lost. Now the rest of the team won't talk to him. What will you do?

1 John 3:16-18

Your friend gets into trouble a lot after school. You like him, but you don't want to get in trouble. When he asks you over to his house, what do you say?

1 John 3:16-18

You heard your best friend laughing when a group of popular kids were making fun of you. What do you think about what your friend did? What can you do and say?

1 John 3:16-18

You worked for two weeks to get to the next level in your computer game. Then your sister played the game and didn't save your score. Now you will have to start the game at the beginning again. What will you say to your sister?

1 John 3:16-18

Two of your friends sometimes do things that get them into trouble. Your parents won't let you spend time with them, but you really like them. What do you say when they ask you to go to the mall with them?

1 John 3:16-18